What can I do with...

a Teaching Qualification

Other titles in the series:

trotman

What can I do with...

a Teaching Qualification

Catherine Maguire

What can I do with… a teaching qualification?
This first edition published in 2004 by Trotman and Company Ltd
2 The Green, Richmond, Surrey TW9 1PL

Editorial and Publishing Team
Author Catherine Maguire
Editorial Mina Patria, Editorial Director; Rachel Lockhart,
Commissioning Editor; Anya Wilson, Editor; Erin Milliken,
Editorial Assistant
Production Ken Ruskin Head of Pre-press and Production
Sales and Marketing Deborah Jones, Head of Sales and Marketing
Managing Director Toby Trotman

Cover design Pink Frog Ltd

British Library Cataloguing in Publication Data
A catalogue record for this book is available from the British Library

ISBN 0 85660 865 3

Typeset by Mac Style Ltd, Scarborough, N. Yorkshire
Printed and bound in Great Britain by Bell & Bain Ltd, Glasgow

Contents

About the author

Catherine Maguire is a Careers Adviser at London Metropolitan University where she specialises in supporting students on initial teacher training courses.

On completing a secondary PGCE in Social Science in 1994, she taught Sociology and Health and Social Care in a sixth form college for four years. Since leaving teaching, she has completed an MA in Social Research and Evaluation and has managed a variety of projects in the voluntary and higher education sectors to encourage undergraduates and graduates to train as teachers.

Acknowledgements

I am grateful to all the case study participants for taking the time to share their experiences of changing careers. I would particularly like to thank Jane Jones, Anwyn Stephenson and members of the Group for Education in Museums for their suggestions and assistance in finding willing participants.

Introduction

Are you considering embarking on a new career? You are not alone!

The focus on problems of teacher recruitment and retention within the media and among politicians might suggest that teachers are the only professionals who ever consider changing career. Indeed, the Centre for Education and Employment's analysis of resignations from schools in summer 2001 found that one in five teachers resigning from teaching posts were leaving the profession.

However, teachers are not the only people who change career. Research carried out by the Penna, Sanders and Sidney consultancy in 2001 suggests that 60 per cent of workers would or might change careers tomorrow. Graduates are now less likely to remain in one career and a Chartered Institute of Personnel and Development (CIPD) study of 732 human resources practitioners found that recruiters increasingly value experience and performance gained in a range of business units and organisations. Given that the workforce as a whole has become more fluid and mobile, it is no surprise that teachers are also seeking to change career.

However, there is not much information available to help teachers who are planning to make a career move out of teaching. This book will help you make an informed decision about leaving – or remaining in – the teaching profession.

Before you embark on your career change, you need to reflect on why you are considering changing careers in the first place. The Centre for Education and Employment's research suggested that the main reasons teachers leave are: workload; government initiatives; salary; stress; status/recognition and pupil behaviour (secondary teachers). These were all seen as more important than 'career prospects', but thinking about career development needs to be a central part of your search for a new career.

As you read on, you will discover that it is not possible to generalise about ex-teachers' destinations: they work in a wide variety of roles, from customer services managers to new-media professionals, from researchers to senior civil servants. While many still work within the public sector, others can be found in the private sector or running their own companies. You will also see from the case studies that many former teachers have moved around the job market in the years since they left teaching. In fact, you can learn as much (if not more) from these ex-teachers' career *paths* as their current positions. The careers focused on in this book do not form an exhaustive list of options. Clearly, then, former teachers can be successful in a range of careers. But how did they get there and, more important, how can you join them?

Myths and facts 1

What's it like out there? Is the grass greener on the other side?

Myth

The hours won't be as long, the stress won't be as high.

Fact

… but neither will the holidays (although many ex-teachers have said that they didn't need as much annual leave in their new jobs). Teachers work incredibly hard: but so do people working in other roles. Recent research by the Department for Trade and Industry shows that people in Britain have the longest working hours in Europe, with one in six employees working over 60 hours per week. In addition, research by the Economic and Social Research Council (ESRC) in 2001 suggested that long hours are an integral part of working life for those with higher-level qualifications.

Myth

The pay will be better.

Fact

Teachers' pay has, quite rightly, improved a great deal in the past couple of years. While private sector pay has fluctuated with the economy, public sector pay has increased. Information from various sources, including totaljobs.com (July 2003), the Chartered Institute of Library and Information Professionals, and Bookcareers.com (autumn 2003) indicates the following industry salary averages:

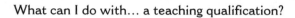

What can I do with... a teaching qualification?

★ Human Resources – Personnel Officer: £22,019–£26,615
★ Public Librarian: £16,944–£24,726
★ Museum Education Officer: £14,000–£25,000
★ New Media – Web Developer: £21,681; Web Designer: £25,321
★ Publishing Sales Executive: £23,439-£29,202
★ Customer Service Manager: £29,177
★ Scientist: £25,670

Local government pay (outside London) for employees with higher-level qualifications ranged from £24,048 to £29,835, with middle managers earning between £29,835 and £35,934. The case studies in this book reveal more information about the salaries of ex-teachers. However, what is striking is that many people leaving teaching had to take an initial pay cut. Also remember that teachers' terms and conditions of service are very favourable in terms of holiday, maternity and paternity leave, sick pay and pension.

Myth

Management experience in schools will guarantee a management position in another organisation.

Fact

There is no guarantee, especially at the start of your career. A recent article on the Chalkface website rather bluntly stated that there was 'no way on earth' that teachers would walk into a management job without further training. While this may be an overstatement, particularly as far as members of the schools' senior management teams are concerned, it is important not to have inflated expectations. You will certainly have a better chance of gaining a management position within the education sector than outside it, and your people-management experience and leadership skills gained from teaching may well help accelerate your career once you have proved yourself in your new job.

Myth

My skills and experience speak for themselves.

Fact

They do not! It is up to you to prove to potential employers that your skills and experience are transferable (see Chapter 2).

Myth

I will gain more respect and status in another career.

Fact

Possibly. Speak to your friends and family about whether *they* feel they have respect and status in their careers.

While the experience of being a teacher will be of great value to you in your future career, some jobs will require retraining. The careers looked at in this book that require retraining include educational psychology, librarianship, accountancy, tax inspection and careers advice.

It is also important to think carefully about whether you might want to return to teaching in the future. DfES figures (January 2003) indicate that in 2000–2001, returners to the profession accounted for 57 per cent of part-time teaching entrants and just under 25 per cent of full-time entrants (although a proportion of these may have been returning after a break to have children). Some of the case studies in this book feature people who would seriously consider a return to teaching: and one of the case study participants has accepted a post as a teacher since being interviewed. If you think you may return to teaching, you need to keep abreast with curriculum and educational policy developments and reflect on what you will be able to offer schools as teacher returner.

What other practical considerations will I need to tackle?

Check with your union about issues concerning resigning after the resignation deadlines (October 31 if you want to finish at the end of the autumn term; February 28/29 to finish at the end of the spring term; May 31 to finish at the end of the summer term).

Transferable skills 2

Why do you want to leave teaching and what else could you do? A successful career change requires serious self-reflection, something that as a teacher you have probably had plenty of practice in.

If the key phrase you keep hearing in your mind is 'escape route', you need to refocus. Career change will only be successful if you begin from a positive and a realistic position. Before you decide to leave teaching, you need to consider whether it is still possible for you to gain satisfaction from teaching. Ask yourself whether it is a change *within* teaching you need rather than a change *out of* teaching.

A desperate career changer is seldom a happy and successful career changer. You need to review what you want from a new career, not just what you want to leave behind. What aspects of teaching would you like to see in a new career? Remember, a job that doesn't have the elements of teaching you see as negative may also lack the positive ones. By concentrating on what you don't want in a job you risk disappointment in two ways:

★ in the selection processes – those negative vibes will show up under the spotlight in an interview situation
★ in your new career – because you only realised what you wanted from your new career when you discovered you weren't getting it.

You should start by looking at the aspects of teaching you do and don't enjoy and analysing the factors that led you into teaching in the first place.

Identifying your likes and dislikes should give you some idea about what you are looking for in a job and whether the factors that brought you to teaching are still important to you now. To move on to the next stage of your career-changing journey, you need to analyse your skills, experience, knowledge and values.

Your *skills* underpin your career development, so skills analysis is vital when changing careers, particularly if your experience as a teacher does not directly relate to the new career you have in mind. Your *experience* is the flesh on the bones of your skills. We can all claim to have skills, but we need to be able to back up our claim with evidence based on our experience.

You have undoubtedly developed and enhanced numerous skills during your career. However, don't assume that potential employers will automatically know what these are as soon as they see 'Teacher' in the work experience section of your application form. Similarly, stating that you have been able to manage a class of thirty 15-year-olds during a Chemistry practical or that you co-ordinated the school's Christmas concert will mean very little to the selection panel for a marketing consultant post, unless you put these statements in the context of the skills the selection panel are actually looking for.

Let's have a look at skills that employers might be looking for; and at what you might have to show for yourself.

Mental Capacity

Dealing with Problems

This includes: identification; analysis; finding solutions; making decisions.

As a teacher you will have observed and made judgements drawing on information from many sources. Many of these decisions will have been made very quickly and sometimes in a pressurised environment.

Information Handling

This comprises: enquiry; research; numeracy; interpretation and analysis; evaluation; and reaching conclusions.

Teachers are constantly analysing and evaluating – whether pupils' performance or the relevance of materials and information to be used in lessons. Those with managerial responsibility will have done this on a larger scale – looking at the performance of a department, a year group or an entire school.

Creativity and Innovation

These are key skills for a successful teacher, from developing exciting and motivating lesson plans while still meeting national requirements, to developing whole-school strategies such as anti-bullying initiatives.

Generic Skills

Verbal and Written Communication

Communication is at the heart of what you do as a teacher. You should be expert in adapting your verbal and written communication methods to suit your audience (pupils with different needs, parents, colleagues, Ofsted inspectors, LEA advisers, etc). You may also be experienced in using IT to enhance your presentation skills.

Teamwork and Leadership

This may include negotiation and 'persuasion'; assertiveness; sensitivity and empathy.

You will have worked in partnership with your teaching colleagues (preparing and sharing resources and monitoring pupils' progress) and non-teaching colleagues such as educational psychologists, learning mentors and learning support assistants. You will also have shown leadership skills through this work, particularly if you regularly have learning support assistants working with you.

Motivating pupils to learn requires negotiation and persuasion. If you have encouraged your department or school to adopt a particular approach or experiment with new materials, this demonstrates assertiveness and negotiation skills. Developing pupils' potential, particularly when dealing with sensitive issues, will have demanded sensitivity and empathy.

Have you had any additional responsibilities as a teacher? If so, did you have to deal with a budget? If not, examine your classroom management techniques and how you have dealt with working in a resource-constrained environment.

Self-management

Self-management includes:

★ organisation and time management
★ responsibility, reliability, commitment
★ ability to cope with pressure and confidence to deal with the unexpected
★ self-awareness
★ self-reliance, initiative, drive and energy
★ self-discipline
★ flexibility and adaptability.

These skills should be easy to identify in your work. Moreover, by completing your teacher training and induction year or by successfully applying for threshold pay, you will have had to meet prescribed standards. Teaching, particularly when going through an inspection, requires a great deal of self-awareness, while the pace of change within education will have demanded flexibility and adaptability.

Business Awareness

This can be one of the scariest skill areas for teachers, which is why it deserves careful attention! If you have had management responsibility you can refer to this, but you need to show that you realise that managing a department in secondary school is not the same as being an account manager for an advertising firm, for example.

You need to know about: current trends; competition; impact of economic, social and political factors. You also need to be able to think in a business-like way, to appreciate how businesses/organisations operate and to have an understanding of 'organisational culture'.

You will need to develop your understanding of the sector and organisation in which you are applying for work, and this will require research. Read the *Financial Times* and any relevant professional journals to bring you up to speed. Compare and contrast the culture within a school with what you might find in your new working environment.

Technical Skills and Knowledge
ICT

As a teacher, you will have been using technology in many forms to enhance teaching and learning. Explore how you could use this experience in other roles.

Subject-specific

This might be languages; statistical; laboratory; expressive and creative arts; design; anatomy; sports etc; related to learning and development; childcare.

What can I do with... a teaching qualification?

If you are a subject specialist applying for work in a related area, you need to consider how you have developed your knowledge as a teacher beyond what you learned through your degree. If you are required to have an understanding of learning and development or childcare, you need to analyse how you can apply this away from the school environment.

These skills were taken from various sources about the skills expected of professionals by recruiters (prospects.ac.uk – the UK's official graduate careers website; the Council for Industry and Higher Education; the Association of Graduate Careers Advisory Services). If you have identified any gaps in your own skills profile, it is essential that you consider how you can develop your skills to fill these gaps.

You could consider embarking on a course. Perhaps you need to learn more about the world of work outside teaching by reading relevant professional journals, or maybe you could consider voluntary work or work shadowing. You may well be working long hours, but if you are serious about changing career and you have identified a skills gap, you may have no choice. You could do this extra work in smaller, more manageable chunks. If it is possible, take one evening a week when you actually finish at 4 p.m. Alternatively, could you use a couple of days outside of term-time? By actively seeking out these opportunities, you will also be providing potential employers with further evidence of your determination, energy and drive.

You should now have a clearer idea about your skill set and the experience it stems from. However, it is important to apply this awareness to each job you apply for. Ensure you pay careful attention to the specific details of a role. Carefully scrutinise job descriptions, particularly the person specification, as these will describe the criteria against which you will be assessed.

Your skills audit should have revealed whether you need to bridge any gaps in your *knowledge*. If you are planning to remain in education in some shape or form or will be using your subject this will be less problematic, but you still need to develop your knowledge of the sector in which you aim to work. There are certain jobs – such as educational psychologist or counsellor – for which further study is a pre-requisite, and others – for example in new media – for which further qualifications may enhance your prospects. If you want to move into research you will find it useful to undertake an MEd or a research-based postgraduate qualification.

Values – Ethics, Principles, Work–Life Balance, Priorities

A further important consideration when planning your career move is the *values* you hold. As well as relating to your principles and ethical stance, values also refer to what you expect from your life in terms of work–life balance, whether you are prepared to take a pay cut or accept less favourable terms and conditions, relocate or retrain and so on.

In order to thrash out these considerations, it may be useful to consult a careers professional in your local authority. If you live or work in London you could make use of the University of London Careers Service's 'C2' service, which provides graduates and professionals with careers consultations. Have a look at their website (www.careershop.co.uk) for details of their services and fees. If you completed your teacher training in the last few years or have recently studied for another qualification, your institution's careers service may still be able to see you, particularly during university vacation times. As well as giving you independent guidance, they will provide you with access to computer packages such as Prospects Planner and Adult Directions to help you focus your career development.

3   Employers' views

The employers who contributed to this chapter have all had experience in working with teachers. Their views offer an important insight into what employers may expect of you, as well as the challenges ex-teachers face and the rewards they gain when changing careers. All of them echo the points made earlier about the need to step out of the box, applying and extending your knowledge, experience and skills to a new environment.

The Careers Professionals

Richard Gledhill is Head of Careers, Nescot College of Further and Higher Education;

Elaine Graham is Director of Careers Service in a Higher Education Institution in Eastern England.

Both Elaine and Richard taught before embarking on careers in human resources, training and development and educational project management.

Having been a teacher, recruited teachers and now working alongside former teachers who are working as Connexions PAs, Richard believes teachers have a great deal to offer. He says:

> 'Teachers' skills are invaluable and I have worked with some fantastic Connexions Personal Advisers who have teaching backgrounds.

> 'It is important to be positive and know what you want. You need to particularly develop your self-marketing skills, especially in the selection process, and make sure you are able to network and adapt to new environments.'

Similarly, Elaine advises you to think seriously about whether you need to change career or just change school.

'Look at other careers in education where your skills and experience will be directly relevant. If you decide on a drastic career change, be flexible – be prepared to retrain, take a salary drop and take short-term contracts.'

Elaine's own career path has seen her taking a number of short-term project-management roles and she suggests that it may be worth taking a risk and accepting such temporary contracts to 'develop management skills and experience'.

She also says: 'believe in the skills you have developed as a teacher as well as the profession itself – don't put down your experience, skills and the profession.'

The Human Resources Director

Tim Williams is Human Resources and Customer Service Director at Edexcel, which is responsible for the provision and assessment of both general and vocational qualifications in the UK and internationally. The organisation, now part of Pearson plc, employs around 950 members of staff, of whom approximately 20 per cent are former teachers. The roles that former teachers undertake tend to be linked to subject specialisms within either assessment (including commissioning exam papers, training markers, collating answers, grading) or qualifications development (writing syllabi/specifications).

What is Tim looking for in new recruits?

'We look for staff who can live up to our values (integrity, teamwork, customer focus and people development) as well as any technical or professional expertise that they bring. Our expectation would be for a professional application as we would expect from a non-teacher, i.e. a good CV, or completed application form backed up by good references when requested.

'We use competency-based questions on application forms, which gives candidates the opportunity to detail how they have demonstrated these attributes in the past. Managers are trained to look broader than subject specialism when they recruit.

'We would expect any applicants to have done research into our business and the role that they are applying for. We are now an overtly commercial organisation (as we are part of Pearson plc). Teachers need to approach working for us with a different mindset. They must also demonstrate that they want the job they are going for rather than that they don't want the job they've got.'

Tim emphasises that former teachers need to prepare themselves psychologically for a change in organisational culture when they leave teaching. While he describes the former teachers with whom he works as, 'the most intelligent, articulate, logical and methodical workforce I have ever worked with', he points out that to succeed, they need to 'think wider than a particular subject specialism, build networks and have a clear understanding of customer service.'

'It can be problematic if teachers have the attitude that working for Edexcel will be more of the same, an extension of school – it is not! The organisation is larger and its way of working is very different. It is important to understand the organisation in the broadest sense – how it works as well as its functions.'

Tim also urges you to consider the impact of a career change on your life as a whole.

'Terms and conditions will be different with pay based on performance and no final salary pension guarantee. Teachers need to think about what they want out of life when they are making the decision to leave teaching in terms of balancing the dimensions of both employment and lifestyle.'

The Museum Service Education Manager

Diana Marks is responsible for her service's education team and currently works with five former teachers. The service provides 'hands-on learning' to schools, offering loans boxes, classroom and gallery sessions as well as advice and INSET training to teachers about using museum objects in learning environments.

What is Diana looking for in new recruits? She says that teaching experience is important in her department: 'Our Education Officer and Manager positions require a working knowledge of the National Curriculum and familiarity with the work of schools and classroom practice.' However, she points out that, for staff who deliver sessions to schools within the museum, 'it is more important for them to be well trained in good presentation skills, with a good knowledge of the museum collection they are working with, and to be approachable and friendly.'

Like Tim, Diana stresses that teachers need to be able to adapt to a new working environment and culture. She stresses that you need to be clear that roles within museums extend beyond teaching schoolchildren and that you do not generally have the opportunity to watch the clients you work with grow and develop.

'Many positions will also include managing other staff and contributing to the general running of the museum in other areas such as ordering and selling in the museum shop, working with museum collections, depending on the size of the organisation. Positions such as education manager will expect individuals to contribute towards general policy or strategy of museum management.

'Teachers also do need to be aware that they may be leading on learning in its broadest sense within the museum, covering families, individuals, all-age groups, schools, foreign language groups – lifelong learning strategies. They may need to be able to show evidence of working that will have given them experience of out-of-school activities. This may have come from voluntary work, working with governors and Parent Teacher Associations.'

Education and support outside the classroom

Connexions Personal Adviser

Breaking in

Connexions is the government's support service for all young people aged 13 to 19 in England. Some Personal Advisers (PAs) may provide careers advice, while others may provide more in-depth support to help identify barriers to learning and find access to more specialist support. In many cases, PA posts are a combination of both roles. They work in a range of settings including schools, colleges, one-stop shops and community centres.

Qualifications

PAs must have a relevant qualification equivalent to (S)NVQ Level 4: a teacher training qualification is regarded as relevant. In addition to this, PAs are required to work towards the Diploma for Personal Advisers or the Understanding Connexions training programme.

Experience and Skills

The Connexions website states that PAs tend to have backgrounds in careers advice, youth work, health services, social services and youth justice as well as education. Relevant skills and experience gained through teaching include:

★ motivating young people to take education, training and work opportunities
★ understanding and meeting the needs of young people
★ working with young people to overcome barriers to learning

★ working with parents, carers and agencies outside the school setting
★ recording and managing information.

Onwards and Upwards

There are some opportunities for 'upward' progression within Connexions and these may expand as the service develops further. It may also be possible to specialise in a particular type of provision. The experience could also be used as a basis for moving into advice work, HE careers advice or work within the youth justice service, social services or the voluntary sector, but this may require further retraining.

A fully qualified PA can expect to earn around £25,000, although posts within London have recently been advertised on a scale of £26,895–£28,758 plus performance-related pay.

Case Study

Sandra Ratcliffe
Connexions PA, West Midlands

Sandra trained as a secondary Modern Languages teacher. Over a period of 11 years she taught in three schools before leaving teaching in 1998. She also held the posts of Head of German and Duke of Edinburgh Award Co-ordinator. Her first post on leaving teaching was part-time School Careers Adviser.

How did Sandra get there?
In addition to the hands-on nature of teaching, Sandra particularly enjoyed being involved in school trips abroad, exchange visits and co-ordinating the Duke of Edinburgh Award. However, she began to find the routine of teaching increasingly monotonous and also felt that she would not be able to continue to perform at the same level throughout her career. 'I wanted a new career that did not need a second degree that I could train for part time and which would use my skills and experience with teenagers.'

Sandra did encounter some challenges on her way to her first non-teaching post, combining part-time study for her Diploma in Careers Guidance, part-time teaching and bringing up a young family. Her first post was part time and, among other activities, involved face-to-face and telephone individual work with Year 11 pupils, group work in schools and presenting at school parents' evenings.

Sandra is now a full-time PA and is about to embark on the Diploma for Personal Advisers.

> 'I work with pupils at two comprehensive schools and an outreach centre for young mums. I support special needs pupils and 'target group' pupils (those at risk of disengaging) in Years 10 and 11, finding extended work experience placements and helping pupils on alternative curriculum to keep attending. I also do home visits and outreach work for those not attending school.'

In addition to this work, Sandra liaises with FE colleges and employers and acts as a 'duty adviser' for 16–19-year-olds who are not in education, training or employment.

Although Sandra is concerned that promotion opportunities may be limited within Connexions, she still feels that her career can progress further. 'I feel in my present job I have considerably more skills and experience and would not find it as hard changing my job.'

How much of Sandra's career progress is owed to her teaching experience?

An understanding of teenagers and how schools operate have been beneficial to Sandra in ensuring that she is able to maintain a fairly high profile in the schools with which she works. Further useful transferable skills and knowledge are:

★ confidence – to walk into a classroom to find a pupil; to give talks at registration periods and in assemblies; with young people generally
★ organisation – monitoring pupils and meeting deadlines; working quickly and independently; multi-tasking
★ classroom management

★ presentation skills, 'although it's considerably more nerve-wracking talking to adults.'

Is the grass greener on the other side?
In 1998, Sandra's salary dropped from £24,000 as a head of department to £8,000 as a part-time probationary careers adviser at the bottom of the pay scale. She is now earning close to the same salary she was earning as a teacher, but she points out, 'I would have been on a considerably higher salary if I'd stayed in teaching with an advanced teacher qualification.' Sandra also feels that, as a PA, she doesn't have the same status as a teacher within the schools in which she works.

She is also quick to point out the advantages:

★ 'It's a steadier job, not so "frenetic" as teaching, you're not under pressure to perform all the time.'
★ 'It is more varied than teaching, more flexible in that you can organise your own week.'
★ The nature of the work with young people:

'You don't have any hassle or grief from the young people. You can talk to them on a level, as adults, without losing control of their behaviour as in a class situation. I get to find out what happens to young people when they leave school, also I get to know more about them generally – their homes, backgrounds and interests.'

★ 'I don't get as many colds as I don't get so run down and exhausted.'

Sandra's advice
★ Be prepared to retrain and/or gain voluntary experience in another capacity or to take short evening courses.
★ 'Think carefully about which route you wish to take to retrain – either apply for a PA post and do in-house training (PA Diploma or NVQ 4 in Guidance) *or* do a qualification in careers guidance full time over a year. Be aware that distance learning courses might not offer you enough practical experience.'
★ Get involved in extra-curricular activities (such as the Duke of Edinburgh Award) while you are still teaching.

Alternatively, seek pastoral or careers roles such as head of year or careers co-ordinator.

★ Gain experience of skills used widely in other jobs such as IT skills, working with adults, one-to-one work over the phone and in person.

★ 'Consider what you do like about teaching and what you would definitely wish to avoid.'

Project Officer/Worker

Breaking in

Project officer/worker roles are a useful way of gaining experience within education but outside the classroom. Project work may be found within LEAs, Excellence in Cities providers, educational charities and other organisations.

Posts are likely to be advertised in the *Guardian* on Tuesdays and Wednesdays, local and ethnic press, and websites dedicated to voluntary sector or local government recruitment such as www.charitypeople.co.uk and www.lgjobs.com. There can be huge variations in status, responsibilities and pay in these posts. While many posts may be advertised with salaries around £25,000, some are aimed at those with experience at senior-level management in schools and the salary and benefits packages reflect this.

Onwards and Upwards

Project work may be based on temporary contracts attached to specific campaigns or externally funded projects with a finite time-span, so there can be a degree of uncertainty in these roles. On the other hand, there is a lot of flexibility and variety and the work can provide opportunities to network and develop potentially fruitful contacts for future freelance or consultancy work. The fact that project work offers the chance to work independently and lead on a variety of initiatives can be useful in progressing to management positions.

Case Study

Geoff Taggart
Project Officer, Reading Families, Campaign for Learning

Geoff taught from 1987 to 2001, predominantly in Early Years. For five years, he worked part-time on supply contracts and in the Ethnic Minority and Traveller Achievement Grant (EMTAG) field while working towards a PhD.

How did Geoff get there?
In the early stages of his teaching career, Geoff particularly enjoyed working on a daily basis with children and the 'fun, humour and creativity they always showed'. As education seemed to move 'away from learning as a good in itself towards narrow, summative assessment', Geoff felt his enjoyment of teaching declined. With this also came the realisation that his career progression within teaching would be restricted. 'Headship was not a possible route because I disagreed fundamentally with the way education was moving.'

While Geoff wanted to move away from teaching within schools, he committed himself to promoting learning. 'In 1993, I took a part-time counselling course. This helped me work out what was important to me and it gave me a strong sense of my personal priorities. I have never lost touch with or compromised these.' To this end, for the last five years of his compulsory-sector teaching career, he combined part-time supply and EMTAG work with a part-time PhD in Education. In addition to his PhD, Geoff also undertook weekend courses in areas such as accelerated learning and neurolinguistic programming (NLP).

Moving out of teaching but remaining within learning presented some challenges to Geoff.

> 'I wanted a job that fitted with my values. Bearing in mind how little I was prepared to move on this, I was looking within a narrow field of employment – a lot of jobs aimed at ex-teachers seemed to be in IT and sales. I decided to work part-time and retrain as there was very little time available to retrain and look for work while teaching.'

Geoff has been working for the Campaign for Learning, initially part-time, since 2001. The Campaign for Learning works to promote and support learning in families, communities, workplaces and schools. Geoff works with the Campaign's Reading Families Millennium Award Scheme's project providers and describes his work as: 'supporting award winners who run community literacy projects, marketing the scheme nationally and delivering training. I also have particular responsibility for evaluating the schemes.'

How much of Geoff's career progress is owed to his teaching experience?
Geoff is very conscious of the value of his teaching experience to his work in enhancing a range of skills:

★ Relating to a wide variety of people – 'I am able to get on the wavelength of lots of people from the Director of the Campaign for Learning to single mums.'
★ 'A well-formed work ethic.'
★ 'Planning and multi-tasking.'
★ Meeting deadlines – 'teachers tend to have a sense of urgency.'

Is the grass greener on the other side?
As with many ex-teachers, Geoff does miss the 'buzz and energy' of working with children. He is aware that he would be earning more money if he had stayed in teaching and had moved on to the upper pay scale, but he says:

'I feel a lot happier. I am able to discuss things close to my heart. My ideas are being used more and I don't feel taken for granted. I can flag up ideas that can be acted upon and taken seriously.

'I get to work with the great and good of the educational world. I feel as if I am working at the cutting edge of new ways of thinking about learning, for example, I am involved in the Campaign's Learning to Learn project, which could really change the culture of learning within schools.'

Geoff's advice
Geoff stresses that it is important to remain positive about your decision to leave teaching. He also points out that you may

need to take a risk, perhaps combining re-training with part-time or supply work, and accept that it might take a long time to find your niche.

'You may not know what it is you really want to do until you stop and take time to reconnect with what is important to you. Look back at what you've done and what it says about you and where you want to be. Think about what excites you and makes you passionate, engaged and curious.'

Educational Psychologist

Qualifications

A revised training route for educational psychology is likely to be implemented from September 2005.

Until September 2005 you must complete an MSc in Educational Psychology – one year full-time or two years part-time in England, Wales and Northern Ireland, or two years full-time in Scotland. To gain entry to the MSc you require the Graduate Basis for Registration (GBR). To meet this requirement you need to have completed either a Psychology degree recognised by the British Psychological Society (BPS) or a BPS-approved conversion course, details of which can be found on their website. The BPS advises that one year's full-time study is the absolute minimum to achieve GBR. If you have never studied psychology before, two years is a more realistic time frame. In England, Wales and Northern Ireland you also need Qualified Teacher Status (QTS).

From September 2005, you will still need to have GBR, but the QTS requirement will be removed. Training will take three years and it is proposed that Educational Psychologists in Training (EPiT) will be paid a salary of £15,183 (plus £2,566 in London). The host local authority in which the EPiT is based will pay the salary and course fees. Training will comprise centre-based work and local authority placements. EPiTs with teaching experience may be eligible for accreditation of previous learning (APL) which could reduce the number of modules required. More information about the proposed training route can be obtained from the BPS or Association of Educational Psychologists.

Experience and Skills

In England, Wales and Northern Ireland you are currently required to have at least two years' qualified teaching experience (teaching under-19s). However, it has been proposed to remove this requirement in England and Wales for training courses running from autumn 2005. In Scotland you will need at least two years' experience of working directly with young people. The skills and knowledge you will need to demonstrate you have gained from teaching include:

★ an understanding of *how* children learn
★ regard and respect for children as individuals
★ ability to 'hold' children's attention
★ monitoring and assessment of children's work and behaviour
★ excellent verbal communication and interpersonal skills including empathy and sensitivity as well as assertiveness
★ administrative, organisational and self-management skills
★ commitment to CPD (continuing professional development).

Onwards and Upwards

Although MSc and conversion courses are very competitive, there is currently a shortage of educational psychologists in some parts of the country. There are opportunities to take more senior positions such as senior and principal EPs in local authorities, but these can be limited.

The Psychology of Education website states that a main-scale EP will earn between £27,996 and £40,455. There is room to negotiate the point at which you are placed on the pay scale. The salary scale for senior EPs starts at £36,669 and principal EPs are paid up to £51,855.

Case Study

Dr Hannah Mortimer
Freelance Educational Psychologist and Writer, North Yorkshire

Hannah taught in both nursery and comprehensive schools as an unqualified teacher before undertaking a Primary PGCE in 1984. Her first post on leaving teaching was as an Assistant Psychologist in a LEA.

How did Hannah get there?
Hannah's career path is not typical of educational psychologists but is a good example of creative career planning. When she embarked on her MSc there were two providers in England that accepted students without a formal teaching qualification.

Hannah discussed her interest in becoming an educational psychologist with the Principal Educational Psychologist in the LEA in which she was based and was offered four months' work experience as an Assistant Psychologist before embarking on her MSc. She says of the role, 'It took me into a number of LEA primary schools, "screening" seven-year-olds for potential learning difficulties. It gave me practice in assessment and diagnosis.'

Following her MSc, Hannah specialised in early years. In order to gain more credibility, she took a year's unpaid leave to complete her PGCE, from which she gained a great deal, not least the chance to embark on her writing career.

'My tutor asked if I would consider sending some of my assignments to a publishing company. That started my 15 years of writing – now 600-plus articles and 30-plus books – all for early years teachers. I found that the writing brought with it opportunities for project work and training; I gradually went part time as an educational psychologist to allow myself to diversify. Five years ago I went freelance. I now earn the equivalent to a headteacher in a large school.'

How much of Hannah's career progress is owed to her teaching experience?

Clearly, undertaking her PGCE gave real impetus to Hannah's career. The transferable knowledge and skills she gained from both her PGCE and teaching experience include:

★ ability to give realistic and practical advice to teachers
★ development of early years specialism
★ enthusiasm for learning and understanding how children and adults can learn together
★ how to 'benchmark' children's performance when assessing for Special Educational Needs
★ understanding of children's individuality
★ ability to think 'on the hoof'
★ self-reflection.

Is the grass greener on the other side?

Hannah does miss being in a team and also getting to know children over time. However, she describes the variety in her current work as creating a 'wonderful life':

> 'One day I might be writing materials for early years teachers or working on the latest book. The next I might be working with families on a "surestart" scheme … then I will be in a school assessing pupils with SEN or running exam stress groups. The next day might be a clinic, then I might be delivering a keynote lecture at a conference on Saturday!'

Hannah's advice

★ Look at what it is about teaching you enjoy. If it is working with children then educational psychology could be for you.
★ You need to be really keen: 'there is a lot of competitive selection at each stage of becoming an educational psychologist'.
★ For those interested in writing – 'Just go for it! Do not assume that others know more than you do. The trick is to communicate simply and clearly in writing. As a teacher, you are probably already good at that.'

Case Study

Veronica Patterson
Independent Consulting Psychologist

Veronica taught in secondary schools as well as doing peripatetic work within a LEA before leaving in 1996. She qualified as a teacher 30 years before. Her first job on leaving teaching was in a locum educational psychology post.

How did Veronica get there?
Having spent her last six years of teaching working as an advisory special needs teacher, Veronica felt she was more interested in 'the *how* of learning rather than the *what*'. Combined with her enjoyment of study and interest in psychology, she left to take an MSc in educational psychology. She had previously studied with the Open University to gain a postgraduate diploma in psychology whilst still working.

While her age and wider life experience were an advantage in her EP training, Veronica feels they may have been a barrier when she was looking for her first EP post: she took several part-time positions around the country before being offered a post closer to home.

Veronica is now a self-employed consulting psychologist, practising independently and through charities. Most of her work involves meeting parents and children for assessment and intervention work. She also delivers some training and contributes to standardisation work for new testing procedures. Of this role, she says, 'I love my job now - there is probably no better one for me.'

Is the grass greener on the other side?
The advantages that Veronica finds in her current role in comparison with teaching are:

★ the opportunity to get out and about
★ the work is always moving on in terms of new research and ideas
★ greater opportunities for CPD

★ more autonomy and less routine – you can organise your own time, particularly if self-employed.

Veronica's advice

★ Do your research – 'read some *Educational Psychology in Practice* journals produced by the Association of Educational Psychologists (AEP) – they can be more readable than university texts – or log on to the EPNET forum through Yahoo groups to gain some insight into current issues for EPs'.

★ Broaden your experience – 'consider taking a post as an assistant psychologist in a LEA, spend time working with children who are troubled to develop empathy or take a SENCO (Special Educational Needs Co-ordinator) teaching post first to gain a breadth of experience about special educational needs. If this is not possible, log on to the SENCO forum on the Web'.

★ Fine-tune your organisational skills and time management strategies, as the work can be overwhelming at times.

★ Think about how your teaching fits into the larger picture of education and learning: 'the cognitive concepts you are trying to develop in pupils and how they can be generalised across the curriculum and into life and work generally'.

★ Investigate 'solution-focused' work to give direction to your thinking when working with others – 'consultation is a major emphasis within the profession at the present time'.

Educational research

Research Posts

Breaking in

There are a growing number of policy think tanks and educational research organisations that employ researchers. These include:

★ National Foundation for Educational Research (NFER)
★ British Educational Research Association (BERA)
★ European Educational Research Association (EERA)
★ Scottish Centre for Research in Education (SCRE)
★ Institute of Public Policy Research (IPPR).

Qualifications

Your degree and teaching qualification may be sufficient for some research posts. However, postgraduate study in an area related to education, policy or research could well be advantageous.

Experience and Skills

Educational research organisations, teaching unions and think tanks do not exclusively employ teachers to do research. In many cases they will be looking for individuals with research and evaluation experience as well as an insight into policy. You need to demonstrate how you have put your knowledge and understanding of educational research and policy into practice. Ensuring that your postgraduate assignments and theses are applied to educational practice is therefore essential, and it would be a bonus if you can show how your research led to changes in policy and practice, even if on a class or departmental level. In terms of more developmental work, your teaching experience, especially if you have middle management experience, may be useful on its own (see Bethan's case study).

There are now more research opportunities in which schools and practising teachers can get involved (look in *The Times Educational Supplement* for information about tenders for school-based research). Advanced Skills Teachers and those involved in ITT may also discover opportunities for small-scale research. You may also wish to investigate contributing to journals, newsletters, websites and conferences run by teacher associations, such as:

★ Association for Language Learning
★ National Association for Special Educational Needs
★ National Association for Primary Education
★ British Association for Early Childhood Education
★ National Literacy Association.

The transferable skills, experience and knowledge you will need to demonstrate include:

★ application of research techniques such as surveys, interviews, observations and case studies
★ analysis and interpretation of information
★ evaluation of strategies, exam performance etc
★ oral and written communication, particularly oral and written dissemination of information
★ numeracy – statistical and IT-based (e.g., use of SPSS statistical software package).

Onwards and Upwards

Salaries in social research can range from a starting salary of around £20,000 to over £70,000 for research directors in the independent sector. To demand a higher starting salary within educational research, you must ensure that you have the skills, experience and knowledge described above.

Most researchers start as a Research Officer (RO) before moving up to Senior Research Officer (SRO) after a few years' experience. It might be possible to enter an organisation as a SRO if you have considerable relevant experience in the area of research you are working on. Some RO and SRO posts may involve more developmental work rather than primary research, while others provide administrative support to the research process rather than carrying out the research itself.

In larger organisations, some upward progress is possible: to Principal Research Officer and Research Director. These roles may involve the management of larger research projects, submitting bids for funding and editing collections of work. Many research posts are offered as short-term contracts, so it may also be worth considering working as a freelancer once you have begun to make a name for yourself.

Case Study

Barbara Lyddiatt
Research Officer, NFER

After doing a secondary BEd, split 50/50 with youth work, Barbara taught Humanities in a secondary modern school for two years.

How did Barbara get there?
Before training as a teacher, Barbara had a variety of secretarial jobs and ran a part-time youth club. The youth work element of her degree enabled her to work with less able pupils on non-curriculum work in addition to her subject-specific teaching. It was this non-curriculum work as well as out-of-hours sessions and school trips that she particularly enjoyed.

Barbara says, 'I couldn't see the point of many of the "rules" any more than the children did', and she felt this made discipline difficult. She found that she lacked support in her department and decided not to return to teaching once she started looking for work again after taking a break to look after her children.

Barbara has been working as a Research Officer for NFER for over 15 years, and it is a role she thoroughly enjoys.

'I approach schools and colleges to invite their participation in surveys and test development. I spend a lot of time on the telephone, answering queries, cajoling teachers into taking part etc.

'I organise the despatch and checking back in of research materials in a great number of projects simultaneously, keeping accurate records, organising the mailmerge and despatch of thousands of letters each month, using Word, Excel and a dedicated database to manage the records.

'I am also one of a small number of people who use SPSS to draw randomly selected and balanced samples of schools or colleges. I have been involved in trialling and advising our IT people on development of our Survey Admin system.'

Barbara has received a great deal of training on different aspects of IT in order to carry out her role. In turn, she also delivers IT training on a one-to-one basis and through informal workshops to her colleagues at NFER. Additionally, her IT skills are now such that she is developing her own business using IT to manipulate and enhance other people's photos.

How much of Barbara's career progress is owed to her teaching experience?
Barbara feels her Research Officer post at NFER combines both her secretarial skills and her teaching experience. While she feels her secretarial skills may be of more practical use than her teaching experience, she feels it has 'made me more sympathetic to the problems facing teachers and I can visualise their role more knowledgeably than I might otherwise have done'. She also believes that teaching was of immense importance in developing her own personal maturity.

Is the grass greener on the other side?
Barbara describes her current job as 'heaven-sent' and can see no disadvantages in comparison to teaching, although she points out that it was not teaching as much as disciplining that she disliked about being a teacher.

Barbara's advice
Barbara offers encouragement to people interested in work similar to hers. 'Go for it, particularly if, like me, you love computers, talking on the telephone, maintaining accurate records and writing reports.'

Case Study

Bethan Hughes
Senior Research Officer

Bethan taught first- and second-language Welsh in two comprehensive schools for 15 years. She left teaching in 1999.

How did Bethan get there?
Bethan was inspired to train as a Welsh teacher by her own teachers. 'I learned Welsh as a second language and was eager to give something back and teach others.' Over time, Bethan became 'frustrated by the increasing paperwork involved in teaching and the pressure to constantly meet new targets'.

The second school in which Bethan worked was relatively small and she was given several positions of responsibility: Head of Department; Language Co-ordinator; and Head of Year. In her final year she was seconded to her LEA as a LEA Adviser. 'This was a really good career move, both in making me aware of opportunities away from teaching but still in education and in confirming that neither of the next logical steps – becoming a deputy or an inspector – were for me.'

Towards the end of the secondment, Bethan was looking for new work both in and out of teaching. She saw the Senior Research Officer post advertised and applied for it.

'My work involves test and task development for the Key Stage 3 national curriculum tests in Welsh (as a first language). I research and prepare written, oral and oral reading tests as well as a 40-page booklet of stories, articles and poems for schools. I also undertake occasional fieldwork outside this remit.'

How much of Bethan's career progress is owed to her teaching experience?

Bethan's teaching experience was essential in gaining her post. 'No-one but a teacher could do the role. Much of the work involves liaising closely with teachers and I visit schools at least twice yearly.'

Bethan initially found it difficult to identify the skills she gained from teaching. As she says, 'It's easy for teachers to under-estimate the transferability of their skills if they have never set foot in another environment.' The transferable skills she has brought to her research role include:

★ 'multi-tasking without even thinking about it'
★ ability to deal with stress and pressure
★ public speaking and presentation skills
★ people management skills.

Is the grass greener on the other side?

Bethan says,

> 'I find the work so stimulating and enjoyable. There is stress in research work but it isn't as constant as in teaching. I have also found a greater degree of autonomy and flexibility in working practices. I do miss the relationships that I had both with pupils and teaching colleagues – the office environment is very different to the staffroom.'

Bethan's advice

> 'Believe you can change career and list what you do as a teacher and its transferable nature. Use the skills you have as a teacher in interviews – presentation and communication skills as well as the ability to think on your feet.'

In relation to moving into research, Bethan has the following tips:

★ have confidence – 'even if you think you know very little about research, as a teacher you can adapt and learn research skills'
★ 'hone your attention to detail – there is a lot of proofreading and self-editing involved'

★ 'you need to be tough-skinned and be prepared to go back to the drawing board if people don't like your work, ideas and resources.'

Case Study

Joe Hallgarten
Associate Director, Education, IPPR

Joe qualified as a primary school teacher in 1993, and for the next five years taught in three schools, holding the position of History Co-ordinator in two of them. His first post on leaving teaching was as a researcher for the NUT.

How did Joe get there?
Joe's decision to teach was influenced by his background in youth and outdoor work and, like Bethan, he particularly enjoyed being part of the school community, working closely with both children and adults, as well as teaching specific subjects such as History. Nevertheless, Joe felt that some of his values were being compromised by the 'excessive prioritisation of SATs performance'. At the same time, he was supportive of the Literacy Hour, which was being piloted in his final school.

Joe was also finding it difficult to maintain enthusiasm for '25 hours a week of performing', which was affecting his life outside school. In addition, Joe felt that in his final year his enthusiasm for teaching suffered from 'post-OFSTED inertia', after an inspection at the start of the school year.

However, Joe is clear that 'the pull towards research was greater than the push away from teaching'. In his final year of teaching, Joe started an MA in Policy Studies in Education and began to develop more of an interest in policy research. He also thought that it was important to leave the profession at a point when it was possible to leave and return if he wanted to, and 'experience life on the outside before considering moving into leadership roles in schools'.

Finding a job outside teaching was easier than Joe had anticipated. He believed at the time that 'teaching seemed to lack CV credibility. Although it gave marketable skills, it didn't have a marketable reputation.' He was offered the post of Researcher in the NUT's Education Action Zone Unit, a role that combined research, assisting members with queries, supporting committees and organising conferences. During this time he contributed to various NUT publications about Education Action Zones as well as facilitating the 'surviving your first year programme' for NQTs.

Joe moved from the NUT to IPPR, a leading independent think tank, as a Research Fellow and was promoted first to Senior Research Fellow and then to Associate Director, Education. In the four years since joining IPPR, he has led a variety of research projects culminating in a large number of seminars and publications, covering a variety of issues from digital media and education to parent–school relationships, school league tables and the future of the teaching profession. Joe is currently engaged in developing a 'PrimaryLab' with the RSA, an experimental approach to the primary curriculum to offer pupils more choice and autonomy over their learning through a competency-based strategy. He also manages a portfolio of projects focusing on topics such as diversity in post-16 education, exclusions and social mobility.

How much of Joe's career progress is owed to his teaching experience?

Joe believes his teaching experience was regarded as a bonus rather than a requisite at the NUT. He regards the fact that he was also studying for his MA and that he had a degree in politics as being just as important. Nevertheless, he strongly feels that the fact that he can say he was a teacher gives credibility to his work as a researcher. He believes he developed the following transferable skills through teaching:

★ communication
★ organisational skills
★ a methodical approach
★ creativity
★ the ability to work with diverse groups including pupils and parents.

Is the grass greener on the other side?

Joe says he would definitely consider returning to teaching.

'I would consider going back, with a view to headship, because I miss being part of a school community, and because, as a headteacher, it is possible to have an enormous impact on local and national policy and practice. I also think that the next decade could be a really exciting one for primary schools, as they hopefully benefit from a period of greater professional autonomy, and an encouragement to innovate.'

He also emphasises that teachers might find themselves missing the autonomy they have in their work and seeing the impact they have, as well as the sense of community that can exist in schools.

Joe does appreciate the autonomy he has at IPPR and identifies the following advantages of his current role in comparison to teaching:

★ salary
★ freedom to manage his own time
★ family-friendly environment
★ opportunity to meet and work with interesting groups of people.

Joe's advice
Joe feels that in the past few years, people have become more aware of what teachers actually do and that teachers considering changing career should feel more confident as a result. He does, however, suggest that you 'think carefully about whether you need to leave teaching or whether the classroom can still provide you with opportunities to develop yourself with good leadership and the right support from your managers'. He also stresses 'no-one likes a moaner – talk the profession up rather than down and focus on what you want to go into rather than what you want to leave behind.'

Higher education advice, guidance and support

Higher Education Careers Adviser

Qualifications

Postgraduate Diploma in Careers Guidance (normally one year full time but it is possible to study for this while in post).

Experience and Skills

Many HE careers advisers have a background in recruitment or careers advice in other settings. A stepping stone to becoming a careers adviser in HE could be to practise careers advice in a school setting. Teaching may well be viewed as valuable experience, giving the opportunity to develop the following key skills:

★ communication and presentation skills in one-to-one and group situations and with a variety of audiences – students, academics, employers
★ ability to analyse and empathise with clients' needs
★ developing action plans with clients
★ working with limited resources.

Onwards and Upwards

There are perhaps more chances to move onwards than upwards as there are a limited number of managerial posts within HE careers services (but see Chapter 12, on Management). Take the opportunity to work on projects, contribute to professional journals and network with employers to develop your career opportunities.

Salaries tend to range from £21,000 to £33,000 depending on experience and the size and location of the institution.

Case Study

Karla Stone
HE Careers Adviser at a university in the East Midlands

Karla trained as a secondary English teacher and taught in four schools over 10 years before leaving in 1995. Her first post on leaving teaching was as a local authority careers adviser.

How did she get there?

Karla entered the teaching profession as a result of her love of English and her belief that teaching was a worthwhile profession. She enjoyed the opportunity to be creative in teaching and motivating pupils to take the subject further through group and discussion work. She left teaching for a number of reasons including the workload, poor discipline in some schools, and the lack of variety in the timetable.

On leaving teaching, Karla took a year out to do a Diploma in Careers Guidance (DipCG), having discussed opportunities in the field with careers advisers and careers information staff. She was fortunate enough to move straight into a careers adviser's post with a careers company contracted to a local authority in the West Midlands. The role, based in both comprehensive and private schools, gave Karla the opportunity to continue the group work she had enjoyed as a teacher. In addition, she was able to do more one-to-one work with pupils as well as liaising with teachers and employers.

Karla moved to a university careers service in February 2003. She describes her role as follows:

'I have maintained a caseload of individual work with undergraduates, postgraduates and international students. I have also had the opportunity to specialise in working with the university's law faculty, help organise projects and contribute to the preparation of the service's bid to gain Matrix accreditation (the national quality standard for organisations delivering careers information, advice and guidance).'

41

What can I do with... a teaching qualification?

How much of Karla's career progress is owed to her teaching experience?

The transferable skills and knowledge that Karla feels underpinned her career path from teacher to HE careers adviser are:

★ 'ability to facilitate group discussion – I did lots of group work in English lessons'
★ 'timing and pacing of activities and presentations'
★ 'understanding where students have come from before they get to university'.

Is the grass greener on the other side?

Karla feels that her current role has a number of advantages over teaching:

★ variety of challenging tasks
★ staff development – more opportunities to attend training and conferences
★ interaction and teamwork with colleagues
★ clients are more appreciative.

Karla gains tremendous satisfaction through carrying out a role that 'enables students to make their own decisions and take responsibility for themselves. As a teacher you sometimes feel you have all the responsibility for students' success – you often feel you are "carrying" them.'

However, Karla points out that as well as having to fund full-time study for a year after leaving teaching, she took a pay cut when she took her first non-teaching post, and she believes she is probably still earning less than she would have been had she remained in teaching. She also has fewer holidays, which Karla says can be difficult with a young family. Many teachers cite stress as a factor in deciding to leave the profession, but as Karla points out, 'stress exists in all jobs, even if it manifests itself differently.'

Karla's advice

Before Karla embarked on her career change, she talked to other careers advisers. She encourages others thinking of making such a move to consider work shadowing. She also emphasises the need to be realistic about some key issues.

42

★ 'Teachers who go straight into teaching from HE may be quite naive about how organisations work, therefore research the career area in which you are interested.'

★ 'Transferability of skills is a plus, but you may need an extra qualification – consider retraining. Consider your skills in the context of the organisation/sector in which you wish to work.'

★ Unlike teaching, careers work is not prescribed by timetables – 'be prepared to organise your own time and juggle demands'.

University Placement Development Adviser

Jobs such as Placement Development Adviser, which do not require specific qualifications other than a degree, are occasionally offered by HE institutions (check out *Education Guardian*, *The Times Higher Education Supplement* and HE institutions' websites for opportunities). However, these posts may well require industrial or business experience in addition to teaching experience.

Case Study

John Babbage
Placement Development Adviser, Bournemouth University

John trained as a secondary Maths teacher, and taught in two schools over seven years before leaving teaching in 1985. His first post on leaving teaching was as Software Engineer, Plessey (which later became Marconi). John's case illustrates how career change isn't necessarily a 'one-off' occurrence but part of a longer career journey.

How did John get there?
John had a variety of reasons for training as a teacher. He felt the role would be both challenging and interesting and that he would be good at it. The opportunity to 'disappear for the summer' was also appealing. He was disappointed with his second teaching post and he couldn't envisage himself teaching for the rest of his life.

Not having children at the time, John found it fairly easy to make the decision to leave and he handed in his notice before he had found a new job. He wrote to local companies and was offered a post as software engineer for Plessey. The post initially offered less money (and responsibility) than teaching but over the 17 years he spent there, working on a variety of telecommunications projects, he gradually began earning more than he would have earned had he stayed in teaching.

After being made redundant, John deliberated over going back to teaching, visiting a middle school and applying for a teaching post in a further education college. He says, 'I still got a buzz from being in the classroom and probably would have taken the FE job if I hadn't been offered my current post.'

John's role as a Placement Development Adviser has the following elements:

> 'I visit students from the university's business school during their placement year, discussing their development, coursework and any issues they may be facing. My work also requires me to write reports and attend meetings relevant to my role with both employers and academic staff. I am largely able to work independently and when not making placement visits, I mostly work from home, visiting the university approximately twice a month.'

How much of John's career progress is owed to his teaching experience?

While he feels that his success in the aptitude tests for his first post was in part due to the fact that he was adept at the 'mental maths' which Maths teachers use every day at school, he points out, 'I don't think they thought, "Oh, here's a teacher".'

John feels the skills gained through his teaching experience (in combination with his experience at Marconi) were relevant in gaining his current position, despite having been out of teaching for over 15 years. In particular:

★ 'ability to get on well with young people'
★ 'ability to encourage, help and listen'
★ 'presentation skills – especially when required to lead impromptu, off-the-cuff informal discussions.'

Is the grass greener on the other side?

John took a pay cut when he moved out of teaching and another one when he took his current job. However, while he doesn't feel he has ever experienced the same highs he gained from some aspects of teaching, he has found that his role at Bournemouth University is less stressful and also gives him the flexibility to combine his work with family responsibilities.

John's advice

Like Karla, John emphasises the need to carefully consider the steps which are necessary to take when changing career. He has the following advice: 'Don't leave it too late to leave the profession and learn how to market yourself to employers on the basis of the skills you already have.'

John is also keen to point out the need to be realistic in career expectations, particularly in relation to:

★ pay – be prepared for a salary drop
★ status – be prepared to start in a fairly junior position. 'Don't expect to move into a high-powered position just because you are a teacher, especially if the role is not directly related to teaching.'

Higher Education Advice Worker

Qualifications

There are no specific qualifications required for advice work. A degree-level qualification isn't necessary for advice work generally, but it is more likely to be expected in an HE setting. If your job involves working with students on PGCE or BEd courses, a teacher training qualification may also be useful, but it is your experience and skills that are most relevant. There are a variety of qualifications offered in advice work at NVQ and postgraduate level, but most people undertake these courses once in post.

Experience and Skills

Your experience in schools, particularly on the pastoral side, will be relevant. Nevertheless, given that there is some

What can I do with... a teaching qualification?

competition for this work and posts may not be advertised
frequently, it would be an advantage to gain some voluntary
advisory work experience to enhance your prospects.
Relevant experience and transferable skills gained from
teaching include:

★ working within externally set and changing policy
  frameworks
★ working with clients from diverse backgrounds with a
  variety of needs
★ dealing with stress and conflict
★ dealing with people in a sympathetic yet firm manner
★ interpersonal and communication skills
★ flexibility and resourcefulness
★ attention to detail and analytical skills
★ maintaining records.

Onwards and Upwards

As with HE careers work, career development tends to be
more sideways than upwards. You may be given the
opportunity to specialise in a particular type of advice work
(e.g. finance). Alternatively, you may decide to retrain as a
counsellor or move into advice work outside HE, for example
within the health or voluntary sector. Opportunities for
promotion may be found in managing or training other advisers.

Salaries are likely to range from £15,000 to £30,000 depending
on experience and the size and location of the institution.

Case Study

Sam Brown
**Advice and Information Officer (International), London
Metropolitan University**

Sam qualified as a secondary Modern Languages teacher in 1997
and left full-time teaching in 1998. She previously taught English

as a Foreign Language in Japan, Austria and Jersey. After leaving teaching she became an Adviser for International Students and Students with Disabilities at Surrey Institute of Art and Design.

How did Sam get there?
Sam's passion for languages and teaching led her to do a PGCE and she enjoyed being able to fill pupils with enthusiasm. However, she was frustrated both by the national curriculum framework and the constant need to act as a referee rather than a teacher.

Leaving teaching so soon after she started presented Sam with the challenge of explaining to interviewers why she was changing career, but it took only three months to find a job. Both her non-teaching posts have involved:

'providing welfare advice to undergraduate and postgraduate students by appointment, email and telephone in addition to developing Web- and paper-based advice and information. I have also led staff training and instigated strategies to meet the needs of international students in the institutions where I have worked as well as developing and maintaining IT-based record keeping systems.'

How much of Sam's career progress is owed to her teaching experience?
Sam has continued to teach in adult education and was also a deputy director of a charity, illustrating that it can be immensely beneficial to take opportunities in addition to teaching work in order to make oneself more employable.

Reflecting on feedback from clients and in appraisals, Sam feels that the following experience and skills gained from teaching have been particularly valuable:

★ 'ability to use initiative and get things done, multi-tasking and time management'
★ creativity – 'approaching things from a different angle'
★ inter-cultural communication and the 'ability to communicate clearly verbally and in writing to people for whom English is not their first language'
★ report writing and record keeping.

Is the grass greener on the other side?
Possibly because she left teaching relatively early, Sam's found she was earning more in her first post on leaving teaching, and her current salary is more or less on a par with that of a main-scale teacher. There are many aspects of HE advice work that Sam appreciates in comparison to teaching. As well as not having to mark work and deal with discipline issues, they include:

★ freedom to self-manage workload
★ diversity of clients and tasks
★ opportunity to travel
★ being able to have 'switch-off' days.

Sam stresses that:

'HE institutions are much larger than schools, so there tends to be more bureaucracy which can cause decisions to take a long time to be made (or never to be made at all!). Furthermore, like schools, HE institutions are resource-constrained environments and budgets can suddenly be cut drastically.'

Sam's Advice
'Ask to work-shadow someone in the holidays so you get a "real" and not a "rosy" picture of advice and guidance within HE.'

She offers the following tips:

★ 'be prepared to answer questions about why you are leaving teaching'
★ 'carefully research the sector in which you wish to work'
★ 'weigh up the costs and benefits of leaving teaching and entering a new profession – consider aspects such as pensions, holidays and stability.'

Museums 7

Education Posts

Breaking in

There are many education roles in museums, galleries and other sites of interest, including:

★ Museum Education Officer
★ Informal Learning Manager
★ Education Assistant
★ Access and Learning Officer
★ Knowledge Development Manager
★ Education Internet Resources Developer
★ Widening Access Education Officer.

Qualifications

A teaching qualification, and often a postgraduate qualification in museum education, may be required. Such qualifications include the part-time MA in Museums and Galleries in Education at the Institute of Education in London and the University of Leicester's distance learning MA, MSc and Postgraduate Diploma in Museum Studies.

Experience and Skills

Experience gained through the curriculum and extra-curricular activities, and supplemented by voluntary and/or casual work undertaken during holidays and at weekends, is vital. As the emphasis within the sector is on lifelong learning, you will need to demonstrate the ability to support the learning of a range of individuals and groups, including families, older learners, academics and community groups, rather than just

What can I do with... a teaching qualification?

the age range you specialise in as a teacher. You will need to demonstrate the following to potential employers:

★ interest in and knowledge of the site's collections
★ commitment to inclusion and life-long learning
★ creativity
★ ability to plan the use of resources to motivate learning
★ information and communication technology (ICT) skills.

Onwards and Upwards

Posts advertised recently have ranged from just over £7 per hour for casual education assistant posts to about £14,000–£25,000 for officer posts, depending on the size and location of the site or museum. Manager posts seem to be on a scale ranging from £25,000 to £32,000. Posts are increasingly offered on fixed-term contracts.

Career progression may depend on the size of the organisation for which you work. Geographical mobility may be useful, particularly if working for smaller sites. Education manager posts can involve managing teams of education officers, casual assistants and volunteers as well as policy and strategic planning work. There are also some opportunities to contribute to museum education courses, write for journals and offer consultancy services to sites. As with education and learning generally, the use of new media is an increasingly important area of work (see Chapter 10, IT).

Case Study

Lynne Minett
Education Officer, the National Coal Mining Museum for England

Lynne qualified as a secondary History teacher and taught for three years before moving to her current post in 2003. She worked in one school, where she held the position of assistant head of department.

How did Lynne get there?

Lynne was clear from the outset that teaching was part of her career path towards working in heritage education. To this end, she subscribed to the *Museums Journal*, for its recruitment supplement, and engaged in voluntary work. Lynne's efforts paid off and she found work quickly: 'I saw the job when I hadn't really made up my mind and applied on the off-chance I would get it, and did.'

Although Lynne's present job involves weekend work during events such as the National Children's Art Day, her working hours are generally regular office hours. Her work entails the following:

> 'I devise the school programme, writing resources, devising workshops and hosting events. I also develop holiday activities and the relevant marketing material and have input into gallery design and interactives. I meet partner organisations, e.g. Business Education Partnerships, National Grid for Learning and other school or community groups who want to work with the museum, and supervise a team of live interpreters and an assistant.'

How much of Lynne's career progress is owed to her teaching experience?

Lynne has found her teaching experience useful in her current post:

★ 'good knowledge of the National Curriculum, which helps when devising resources and workshops'
★ 'credibility with teachers'
★ 'an insight into marketing and networks'.

Is the grass greener on the other side?

Although she misses the holidays she enjoyed as a teacher, Lynne feels her present post offers these benefits:

★ 'less workload'
★ 'a nicer physical working environment'
★ 'more support'.

Lynne's advice

Lynne suggests that before you move into museum education, you should 'investigate all the options and speak to people who have left. Gain experience of delivering resources or workshops in museums and demonstrate management experience and good knowledge of ICT.'

Case Study

Sarah Gouldsbrough
Schools Development Officer, Durham Studies Department, Durham County Council Cultural Services

Sarah qualified as a primary teacher in 1995 after taking a four-year BEd. She taught in three schools before she left the profession in 1998. In her final year of teaching she was PE co-ordinator. Her first post on leaving teaching was Casual Education Assistant, Bede's World, Jarrow.

How did Sarah get there?
Sarah had wanted to be a teacher for a long time and enjoyed the challenges involved in working with children. Nevertheless, the demands of planning and assessment, a lack of support and a succession of short-term contracts led her to make the decision to look for work within museum education.

'I made the decision to work in museum education during the summer break so I prepared a CV and covering letter and sent it out to all the museums around Tyne and Wear that I could think of. I got several replies telling me to look out for forthcoming jobs. I got one reply from Bede's World in Jarrow, offering me some casual work as an education assistant, leading school parties around the site, doing object handling sessions and helping to develop the education service in general.

'I trained for the work by shadowing colleagues, and taking notes. I was also given all the various teaching packs to help me learn more about Anglo-Saxon life. I was paid just over £5 per hour, and rarely worked more than one or two days a week and some weeks not even that.'

It took Sarah less than a year to find her first post but longer to find permanent work: 'I had to be patient, and build experience with courses, casual and temporary work, before I was able to get a full-time post in January 2000. I had to learn quickly how to sell my teaching talents when I had little museum experience.'

Although Sarah's current post is fixed-term, being on a three-year full-time contract gives her greater security than she had in previous jobs, and she enjoys the benefits of being employed by a local authority.

'I am employed to develop the schools education provision in all its forms for three museums: Durham Light Infantry Museum and Durham Art Gallery; Binchester Roman Fort; and Killhope, the North of England Lead Mining Museum. As there has been no education officer for any of the museums before (apart from an externally funded projects), I am taking on a service that is excellent in parts, but needs a concentrated effort to improve it and take it forward.'

Sarah's tasks include:

★ developing effective marketing tools and better use of the websites
★ developing bids for funding to develop new activities and resources
★ writing policies for learning and access, and developing realistic strategies to accompany them
★ carrying out market research and evaluating existing activities and resources
★ working with school groups
★ developing relationships with partners both within the council and outside it.

How much of Sarah's career progress is owed to her teaching experience?

'I wouldn't have been employed if I hadn't been a teacher due to the nature of the work. Teachers, particularly those on visits, with whom I have worked know, without me telling them, that I have been a teacher and they really appreciate that fact. They know that I understand how schools operate, and how children "work"!'

Sarah regards the following as being particularly useful in developing her career:

★ 'knowledge of the National Curriculum'
★ 'understanding how children learn, and how to plan to facilitate that learning'
★ 'understanding the logistics of schools – timetables, planning, pressures of curriculum, procedures etc'
★ 'having to be creative and have lots of ideas!'

Is the grass greener on the other side?
Sarah is clear that she is very unlikely to return to the classroom, despite earning about £8,000 less than she would be earning had she remained a teacher. She considers her current profession to have the following advantages:

★ 'flexible working day and flexible holidays and not feeling guilty if I am off work with illness'
★ 'I don't have to take work home'
★ 'I am able to travel and work with lots of different people'
★ 'I feel more valued for what I am doing.'

Sarah's advice
★ 'Get some experience – do voluntary work.'
★ 'Send unsolicited CVs – it may get you some casual work.'
★ 'Permanent jobs are few and far between but if you are prepared for temporary jobs and times where you may be unemployed, lots of places run projects funded for set periods and you can gain valuable experience this way.'

Case Study

Clare Carlin
Community Learning Manager, National Trust, Osterley Park House

Clare qualified as a secondary English and Drama teacher in 1996. She taught in one school for six years, where she also held several co-ordinator roles within her department.

How did Clare get there?
Clare enjoyed many aspects of secondary teaching. 'I was never

bored, the pupils were entertaining, lively and challenging.' Towards the end of her time as a teacher, she felt a little 'ground down' by a mixture of the social issues faced by pupils, education's shifting political agenda and the workload she faced.

After four years in teaching, Clare began to research other career options available and looked at museum education.

> 'I knew it wouldn't be a quick move because of the specialist knowledge required. I dedicated a lot of my leisure time to gaining relevant voluntary work experience and completing my MA in Museums and Galleries in Education part-time while still teaching.'

Clare has held her current position since 2002.

> 'I am in charge of all learning and interpreting activities, such as Wartime Christmas at Osterley, within Osterley Park House and its grounds. As I am on my own in this role, I tend to do everything from general administration to encouraging new visitors and developing learning programmes for schools and families.'

How much of Clare's career progress is owed to her teaching experience?
Although Clare ensured she gained a great deal of knowledge and experience in her spare time before changing career, she describes her teaching experience as 'completely relevant' as most of her current work is with schools. She highlights:

★ relating programmes of work to National Curriculum targets
★ using resources
★ classroom management
★ 'understanding teachers and their demands'.

Is the grass greener on the other side?
Clare's salary has dropped by at least £8,000. She also misses the depth of contact she had with students in school, as well as the opportunity to teach literature. In contrast, she notes the following benefits of her present work:

> 'There is more variety in the content of what I do and the involvement with informal education through working with

families, adults and community groups means that activities aren't driven by meeting targets and getting good grades from pupils. I don't experience the grind of classroom management issues and a day's work isn't followed by a pile of marking!'

Clare's advice

Clare advises you to develop both a theoretical and practical understanding of museum education, emphasising the need to ensure you can offer 'concrete experience – otherwise you will just seem to be another teacher trying to get out'.

Case Study

Alison Porter
Freelance Writer and Museum Learning Consultant, and MA Lecturer

Alison taught secondary Science for eight years, holding the positions of Head of Biology and Head of Lower School Science. She then moved into FE, teaching young people with SEN. Her first post on leaving teaching was as Assistant Education Officer, Science Museum.

How did Alison get there?

Alison found teaching very rewarding, particularly 'watching children develop, seeing their enthusiasm and encouraging them to do things they didn't think they could do.' She did not make a conscious decision to leave teaching, but as a way of exploring her options before she progressed further up the management ladder she decided to work for a while in FE. 'I job-shared my teaching post and worked part-time in FE teaching young people with SEN. I also worked as an examiner and youth worker.'

When one of her part-time FE posts came to an end, Alison saw a part-time job writing resource materials for the Science Museum advertised in the *TES*. She stresses, 'it was quite a quick decision, I didn't feel as if I had actually decided to leave. I worked there part-time for about a month and then a full-time post became available.'

Initially her work at the Science Museum involved 'writing resource materials, developing teachers' courses and events, marketing and being involved with all aspects of provision for schools'. Alison quickly became involved with the work across the unit, considering the learning needs of all visitors, through areas as diverse as gallery development, evaluation and workshops. She remained at the Science Museum for 15 years, winning four promotions and eventually being responsible for the services delivered by 70 members of staff. Her role extended to include:

'responsibility for all the unit's work including policy, access and inclusion, the management of training, customer service, resources, events and the development and delivery of some of the museum's most successful galleries including the Garden and Launch Pad.'

During her time at the Science Museum, Alison was also engaged in a variety of other activities which helped pave the way to a successful freelance career:

'I also worked with publishers and provided consultancy to other museums, such as training museum staff in the Czech Republic and Slovakia. I was involved in the delivery of a module on a MA course for teachers at the Institute of Education run in conjunction with the Victoria and Albert Museum.

'During a break from work due to family responsibilities, I became involved in voluntary work and became involved with a charity for looked-after children, of which I am now the chair of trustees.'

Alison is currently involved in a variety of work, from lecturing for the Institute of Education and Open University to providing consultancy to a number of museums. She also writes for a variety of professional journals and magazines, is writing a book and is a consultant for a number of well-known publishers. Over time, her income has increased to more than she would be earning as a teacher.

How much of Alison's career progress is owed to her teaching experience?

Alison believes 'museums are all about *learning*', and that it is essential for museums to employ former teachers.

> 'You never forget the needs children have once you have been a teacher. You have a wide range of very relevant and transferable skills. You may find that they enable you to empathise with visitors, have an insight into their learning and practical needs, plus suggest imaginative and wide-ranging ideas to engage even the most reluctant learner.'

Alison highlights the following aspects of teaching as being vital in museum education.

★ 'Facilitating learning with groups ranging in age, abilities and interest.'
★ 'Teaching in comprehensives in challenging areas is very useful because of the current focus on inclusion in museums. Such practical experience is useful in terms of understanding the issues, plus the delivery and development of strategy.'
★ 'Experience of taking schoolchildren on visits – understanding how they deal with being in a different environment. Many museums need first-hand experience in these areas to fully understand what they could and should offer schools and teachers.'
★ 'Understanding of family dynamics and behaviour.'

Is the grass greener on the other side?

Alison experiences huge variety in her work and thoroughly enjoys the flexibility she has. Despite this she does warn that you may miss the depth of contact you have with children as a teacher.

Alison's advice

As an MA lecturer, Alison often works with teachers interested in moving into museum education. She has also interviewed and employed many teachers in the past and stresses how important it is to visit the museums in which you are interested in working: 'I'm amazed at the number of applicants who come to interviews who haven't looked round the museum!'

Alison's experience has led her to offer the following tips.

★ Be aware of the type of work available. 'Most museums and galleries now have learning posts that focus on *lifelong* learning – families and adults as well as schools – so it is important to demonstrate an understanding of the learning styles and needs of a range of people. You have a wide range of very relevant, transferable skills.'

★ 'Consider your management style as a teacher and how you can adapt it to managing adults – remember they are not pupils!'

★ Take advantage of volunteering opportunities in museums at weekends and during holidays, 'to get a feel for the environment'.

★ Do a part-time MA in Museum Studies alongside teaching. 'Many people start the course I lecture on as teachers and then move into museum work as they progress through the course.'

Information services, publishing and journalism

Linguist – Translation and Interpreting

Qualifications

A degree in the foreign language(s) with which you will be working is of great value. It is desirable for translators and vital for interpreters to have a masters degree or other postgraduate qualification in either translation or interpreting. A list of these courses available in the UK is provided by the Institute of Translation and Interpreting (ITI). The ITI also provides useful fact-sheets about getting into interpreting and translation.

Experience and Skills

Many linguists are able to use more than one foreign language. Some translators and interpreters may have a background in the field in which they will be practising translation or interpreting (e.g. law, engineering or science), while others may be generalists. You must not only be fluent in the relevant languages but also have a good knowledge of the subjects in which you will be involved, as well as the culture of the countries where your other languages are spoken. You will need to demonstrate:

★ total mastery of first language and mastery of *at least* one foreign language
★ understanding of world and commercial issues
★ experience of other cultures
★ memory
★ analysis
★ empathy – both with individuals and with texts
★ flexibility – ability to adapt when subjects and situations suddenly change
★ excellent IT skills.

Onwards and Upwards

Work, particularly in translation, tends to be freelance, although it is not unusual for translators to work initially for translation companies. Freelance work and/or permanent or fixed-term contracts can be found in the civil service (e.g. the Home Office, in particular the Immigration and Nationality Directorate (IND)), EU institutions, NATO and the UN. Not surprisingly, there is huge competition for positions in large international organisations.

Rates for translators are normally charged per 1000 words. Rates advertised on various agencies' and freelancers' websites in November 2003 varied from £40 to £200. Interpreters tend to be paid by the day, half-day or hour.

Case Study

Simone Brooks
Postgraduate Tutor/Legal Interpreter

Simone taught Music and Modern Languages in two schools between 1990 and 1995 and on supply in a variety of schools, both primary and secondary, until 2001. Her first post on leaving teaching was Freelance Translator, European Court of Justice.

How did Simone get there?
Simone enjoyed some aspects of teaching – 'the buzz of contact with children and the creative side of preparing lessons' – but gradually moved away from teaching as she picked up more translation work.

She says, 'translation and interpreting is a very competitive profession and it is difficult to find work.' She feels that she initially lacked the skills to market herself effectively and it took some time to build up her portfolio of work to a level she was happy with.

'I am a freelance linguist and my only "job" (paid by the hour) is as a teacher on an MA interpreting course which I got through a friend. I have found work through contacts and through professional associations and, sometimes, through agencies. Since qualifying as a legal interpreter, I have written directly to courts of law so that they may engage me for assignments. I interpret for defendants in court and, with solicitors, in prison. This includes consecutive interpreting and whispered simultaneous interpreting in court.

'It has taken me around eight years. I have also worked as a bilingual secretary and taken further courses in interpreting, translation and legal interpreting. I have always been self-employed. The main issue this presents is the unreliable nature of the work, but when it is going well, I do enjoy the variety and the freedom. My pay is about the same as when I was teaching but I am earning less than I would be [if I had stayed] in teaching.'

How much of Simone's career progress is owed to her teaching experience?
Of the impact of her teaching experience on her career, Simone says, 'it did not help me to get my university teaching job, but it helped me enormously when I was carrying it out. I have also trained on other interpreter training courses when it has been similarly useful.'

Is the grass greener on the other side?
Simone can see the pros and cons of being a freelance linguist. 'It is less stressful and less intense with more variety, but the translation side of it is isolated. The work is not guaranteed and it is less creative.'

Simone's Advice
Simone encourages you to take a calculated risk in becoming a freelance linguist:

'Only do it if you have a secure financial base; building up contacts takes a long time. Be brave and give it a go – you can always come back to teaching. Even if the career change does not suit you, you will have broadened your experience and will have something to take back into school.'

Hansard Reporter

Qualifications

A good degree is desirable but not essential.

Experience and Skills

Again, relevant experience is desirable but it is more important to have:

★ excellent English language skills
★ a keen interest in current affairs
★ the ability to work varied and long hours.

Onwards and Upwards

Trainee reporters earn from £16,871 to £23,423. On successful completion of the three- to four-month training period, recruits become fully fledged committee reporters. The central focus of the role is to report House of Commons business in an easily understandable and consistent written format. Hansard reporters either sit in the chamber to record debates or report on Westminster Hall and Standing Committees. Career progression may see reporters becoming committee room sub-editors. Further up the career ladder are Principal Assistant Editors, three Deputy Editors and the Editor of the Official Report.

Case Study

Richard Purnell
Hansard Committee Reporter, House of Commons

Richard qualified as a French and Spanish teacher in 1998. He taught full-time until July 1999 and on supply until March 2003. His first post on leaving teaching was as a translator/ abstractor for FT.com.

How did Richard get there?

When Richard moved into teaching, it was because he felt 'it was time to become a proper teacher' after teaching English as a foreign language abroad. He enjoyed 'the feeling of being central to children's lives', but was unhappy with the 'prevailing methodology' of language teaching as well as discipline issues and bureaucracy.

It took Richard five months to find work outside teaching, using a variety of job-search strategies. 'I registered with some agencies, wrote unsolicited letters to certain companies and scoured the creative and media jobs section of the *Guardian* on Mondays. I also used and registered with job-search websites such as monster and jobsunlimited.'

Richard's first post was on a night shift at FT.com.

'My work involved selecting important business articles from the websites of French, Spanish and Belgian newspapers and writing a summary in English of 25 of them. The pay was £17,600 per year, which I supplemented by supply teaching.'

Richard has just finished the three-month Hansard Committee Reporter training and is earning a salary of £22,000, which he estimates is about £6,000 less than he would be earning if he had continued teaching.

'The daily work involves transcribing speeches/interventions from the Standing Committees and proceedings at Westminster Hall. We do not transcribe word for word, but write a substantially verbatim report of what was said, omitting redundancies, correcting grammatical errors and conforming to Hansard style. Hours are irregular and vary according to parliamentary business.'

How much of Richard's career progress is owed to his teaching experience?

Richard felt that his teaching was largely irrelevant. When applying for jobs he sometimes got the impression that 'employers – unfairly, in my view – thought that teaching did not constitute "real world" experience'. Despite this, he considers that, 'because teaching involves such a range of challenges, bureaucratic, interpersonal, organisational and so on, my teaching experience was relevant, at least in some ways, to the jobs I was applying for.'

Is the grass greener on the other side?
Richard misses the 'intensive human contact of teaching' and the opportunity it afforded him to use his languages. Despite this, he feels his current post has the following advantages over teaching:

★ 'more interesting and focused work'
★ less bureaucracy
★ 'fewer simultaneous pressing demands'.

Richard's advice
Richard suggests that any teacher planning on changing career should 'talk up the versatility that teaching demands at interviews'. Like other former teachers, he stresses how important it is to recognise that you may have to accept a pay cut or 'humbler' company position on changing career. He suggests using supply work to 'relieve you of any financial pressure to get a job quickly and free you up to look thoroughly for a job you really want'.

If you are interested in training as a Hansard Committee Reporter, Richard emphasises that it is necessary to 'be interested in and knowledgeable about politics and be able to write coherently, with good grammar'. He also underlines three key things that you need to be prepared for:

★ 'a drop in salary, at least initially'
★ 'more irregular working hours'
★ 'role reversal – *you* will be the pupil at the beginning'.

Librarianship

Breaking in

Library professionals can work for schools, colleges, universities, professional bodies, subject associations and government institutions as well as public libraries.

Qualifications

You will need to take a postgraduate qualification in librarianship or information management. The Chartered Institute of Library and Information Professionals (CILIP) has details of courses it accredits.

Experience and Skills

You will need to gain up to one year's experience of working in a library or information management work to be accepted on to a postgraduate course, particularly if studying part-time or via distance learning. Experience in a school library could be extremely valuable. Voluntary work in a resource centre or library may also be beneficial. Another possible route is to combine supply teaching with part-time library work.

Graduates with little relevant experience may be eligible to undertake training through CILIP's Library and Information Management Training Opportunities scheme (but expect fierce competition). This scheme offers graduate career changers a year's training in a library or information management setting (such as a tourist information centre or resource centre) in order to gain the experience necessary to embark on relevant postgraduate study. In some cases trainees may be kept on throughout their course.

Skills relevant to professional library work that you will have developed as a teacher include:

★ strong IT skills
★ selection and organisation of resources
★ ensuring resources are accessible to clients
★ confidence in working with and presenting to groups and individuals.

Onwards and Upwards

The obvious point of entry for former teachers is school or college libraries; but your postgraduate qualification can enable you to work in any library setting. Another career option might be information management. Closely allied to librarianship, this is a career area also encompassed by CILIP's work.

Librarians' salaries do not compare particularly favourably with teachers' salaries. CILIP's recommendations for public librarians' salaries for April 2003 to March 2004 range from £16,944 to £24,726, rising to a minimum of £23,358 for specialists and £40,000 for Local Authority Head of Library (and Information) Services posts. Posts in London currently attract an additional allowance of £2,847 (Inner London) and £1515 (Outer London).

Case Study

Emma Ratcliffe
County Council Lending Stock Specialist

Emma qualified as a Religious Studies teacher in 1996. Her first post on leaving teaching was as a library assistant.

How did Emma get there?
Although she enjoyed working with children, Emma felt frustrated at 'not being able to meet my aims in the classroom due to discipline and the general ethos of the school'. She left the profession shortly after qualifying.

> 'I was young and thought that if I stayed, the job may become a trap from which I couldn't escape. I decided that it was a career that I could come back to in the future, but that I had to explore other paths away from the classroom for my own personal development. [I wanted] to increase my knowledge of the world and to find something else that would enable me to develop in other directions.'

What can I do with... a teaching qualification?

Emma did not receive any professional help in finding a job outside teaching and used the local and national press to search for work. It took her two months to find work, although she regarded her first post as a library assistant as a temporary measure. During this time she realised that 'the kind of remuneration that I might expect would be significantly less for most other jobs, for a considerable length of time'.

Emma's first post was a gateway to her career development, although her path was not without challenges:

> 'I worked as a library assistant while studying part time for a professional library qualification. This was hard as I had to do this in my own time and pay the fees. After about two and a half years on a clerical grade I was then able to apply for a professional post. My first professional post was as a generic librarian in a town library and was a varied introduction to the profession. I then submitted a professional development report and became Chartered.

> 'After about two years as a librarian I had two children and then returned to work on a part-time basis. The county council has very flexible working patterns which enabled me to find the best option to suit my circumstances. I remained part-time until September 2002 when I was appointed to my present post. In the interim I gained ICT qualifications and dabbled in adult education, being employed as a LearnDirect tutor for a while. This had significant advantages when applying for promotion and enabled me to be confident in an area which many people find difficult.'

Her current role as a lending stock specialist involves, 'selecting and managing the stock in ten libraries and a mobile library. This includes children's books, adult books, videos, DVDs, CDs and software. I also organise and manage stock promotion and children's activities.'

How much of Emma's career progress is owed to her teaching experience?

Although Emma had to retrain and re-qualify as a librarian, she feels her teaching experience helped her develop communication and interpersonal skills; and her background in an educational setting was also beneficial.

Is the grass greener on the other side?
It has taken Emma some time to make up the difference between her pay as a teacher and as a library professional. Nevertheless, she is sure of the benefits of her current role.

> 'Where do I begin! One of the first things that I noticed was that there is no carry-over in most jobs – you don't tend to bring work home with you. You get paid for the time you put in and are not expected to work without pay. I enjoy the adult interaction in my present role, whereas teaching is quite isolated – you are on your own in the classroom.'

Emma's advice
Emma has the following tips for anyone interested in library work.

★ Compared to teaching, librarianship is a small profession and therefore there are fewer opportunities at every level so geographic mobility is a significant factor in ensuring a satisfying career.
★ Ultimately, most jobs will involve managing people or money.
★ Check out the anticipated rates of pay before spending time gaining qualifications.

Publishing Account Manager

Breaking in

The publishing sector is very broad, incorporating books and journals, magazines and newspapers, online services, consumer and business directories as well as public and not-for-profit organisations. There are various roles in publishing aside from editorial work, for example in sales and marketing. Account management roles tend to involve a lot of travel, so it is important to be relatively mobile and be prepared for overnight trips.

Qualifications, Experience and Skills

Experience and skills are probably more important than qualifications. If you are aiming to work for an educational publisher, your teaching qualification will be of interest to potential employers but it will not guarantee you an interview.

It is important to be able to demonstrate an understanding of the market (from being part of the market) and of the products you will be promoting. Experience in the area of publishing in which a firm specialises could be an advantage, whether it is generic education, careers education, new fiction, languages, science and technology, etc. Ensure you are up to date with current trends in the publishing field in which you might be interested.

Knowledge and experience of a particular publishing field are only part of the story in terms of account manager positions. As with similar roles outside publishing, you need to show you have the ability to promote and persuade. You also need to be willing to travel frequently. Recent advertisements for account manager and sales executive roles within publishing have asked for:

★ excellent communication
★ strong leadership
★ training and coaching abilities
★ organisational skills
★ professionalism.

Onwards and Upwards

The obvious route into publishing account management and sales is through educational publishers or those that specialise in your subject specialism. Many firms are quite small, so you may have to change companies to progress.

More senior roles may involve taking on larger clients, managing a team of account managers or becoming a sales representative or sales director. Experience and skills gained in publishing may also be useful for moving into account management roles in other sectors. Progression might be enhanced by taking the Institute of Sales Promotion's (ISP) Diploma and/or other courses.

In bookcareers.com's 2002 salary survey the sector's average salary was £22,655. Salaries are highest in on-line publishing and lowest in audio publishing. The average sales representative's salary was £23,439, whereas for sales managers the average was £29,202. Sales executive and account manager roles advertised on the *Publishing News* website in autumn 2003 had salaries of £21,000–£34,000. The extensive travelling involved in some roles means that packages are likely to include car allowances. As with many posts within sales, bonus incentives are also often offered as part of salary packages.

Case Study

William Maidlow
Account Manager, Trotman Publishing

William trained as a secondary History teacher in 1973, and taught in five schools over the next 27 years. During this time he also held the post of Careers Co-ordinator.

How did William get there?
William became a teacher in order to be able to teach History and he gained a great deal of satisfaction from this, particularly at A-level. He also enjoyed the pastoral and extra-curricular activities he was involved in. However, the constant flow of curriculum and policy changes within education led him to feel:

'I did not want to spend the remainder of my teaching career becoming increasingly negative about a job from which I had derived great satisfaction. In particular I wanted to develop my involvement with careers guidance. I had, of course, also considered moving to a different school, so I was open minded about leaving teaching – needing a change was probably uppermost in my mind.'

71

What can I do with... a teaching qualification?

William's careers co-ordinator role had a direct influence on his move out of teaching. 'My present post with Trotman Publishing was advertised in *Trotman News*, which is mailed to all careers co-ordinators, and it happened to land on my desk when I was considering my options.'

Although gaining a new job seems to have been straightforward for William, he does highlight some challenges he faced when making the decision to leave teaching.

> 'After 27 years' teaching you do get a bit conditioned to life in a school. I did wonder how I would adjust at 50+ to a job in the big wide world. To some extent, as a Careers Co-ordinator I had always had contacts with the world "out there", but working in it for real is altogether more serious. I was concerned (and still am) about my pension position, which is guaranteed as a teacher. I wondered how I would cope with new demands, and whether I would have the appropriate skills.'

William took up his post at Trotman as soon as the school term ended.

> 'My present job requires me to visit customers in careers companies, Connexions Partnerships, adult guidance organisations, and careers co-ordinators in schools and colleges. My job is to discuss their resources needs for careers guidance and identify how Trotman Publishing can help to meet those requirements.

> 'The job is extremely varied, takes me from one end of the UK to the other, and while the hours involved are certainly no less (and often more) than when I was teaching, I do have a lot more control over what I do.

> 'We operate very much as a team, and though I am remote from the company's base in Richmond, I report regularly to colleagues by phone and email, and always receive excellent support from other members of the Trotman Publishing team.'

William has also found the change in career extrinsically satisfying. 'My salary in teaching was matched, and I have been able to continue with the MA I started as a teacher.'

How much of William's career progress is owed to his teaching experience?

Although he admits he was not initially aware of the relevance of the broader skills he had developed as a teacher for his current roles, he now regards them as being extremely relevant:

'The skills I have acquired over the years as a teacher have been extremely valuable. Such skills have assisted me to make presentations, organise exhibitions and displays, communicate effectively with customers face to face, by email and by phone, and to write reports and summaries that are clear and concise.

'Being self-critical, and always seeking ways to evaluate and improve performance and delivery is also something teachers do most of the time. I would add that the general skills I have acquired as a teacher have enabled me to make the transition perhaps more smoothly than I expected.'

Is the grass greener on the other side?

Although William has concerns about his pension and misses teaching History and being in a school environment, he is able to identify many advantages in his current role, which provides 'close support and plenty of motivation'.

★ 'Although I have to respond swiftly to urgent requests, the disruptions are less frequent, and more understandable.'
★ 'The teamwork is genuinely impressive.'
★ 'Meetings are more constructive, and more disciplined.'
★ 'I now get to see parts of the UK I have not visited, I see friends and relations more often and I can arrange my time to suit myself and the company. If I have to travel on a weekend to attend a meeting, I can take time in lieu – and it's really nice to have a day off in the week when everyone else is working.'

William's advice

'Go for it – but only if you have positive reasons for making the change.' As with other case study participants, he emphasises that it is important to focus on the positives of teaching rather than the negatives.

Newspaper Journalism

Qualifications, Experience and Skills

It is possible to enter newspaper journalism as a 'direct entrant' and receive training on the job. The National Council for the Training of Journalists (NCTJ) suggests that the possibility of taking this route is greater for those with relevant knowledge. For a teacher, this may point to educational publications such as *The Times Educational Supplement* and *Education Guardian*. Some papers will also be prepared to allow you to undertake a journalism course by day- or block-release once you have worked on the paper for a while. There are also a variety of NCTJ-accredited full-time postgraduate and (S)NVQ Level 4 courses throughout England, Scotland, Wales and Northern Ireland, including a number of shortened 'fast-track' courses that last for 18–20 weeks.

The NCTJ highlights the following skills as crucial in succeeding in newspaper journalism:

★ an interest in current affairs
★ an interest in people, places and events
★ an ability to write in an accessible style
★ good spelling, grammar and punctuation
★ flexibility – working irregular hours and being under pressure
★ determination and persistence.

You may find it useful to contribute to the journals of the professional associations mentioned in Chapter 5, Educational Research, to increase your chances of impressing editors.

Onwards and Upwards

Posts available within newspaper journalism range from reporters to sub-editors and editors. Freelance work is common and often straddles magazine, broadcast and, more recently, online media.

Salaries for newspaper reporters with a relevant postgraduate qualification tend to start from around £20,000, rising to £40,000 for senior reporters and sub-editors and over £100,000 for national editors.

Case Study

Fiona Flynn
Editor for New Teachers, *The Times Educational Supplement* (*TES*)
Fiona was a primary school teacher and supply and peripatetic EAL teacher from 1994 to 1999.

How did Fiona get there?
Fiona got a great deal of satisfaction from teaching: 'I loved it! I loved camping it up in the classroom and seeing kids' success.' Although her enjoyment was undermined by 'being told what to do and how to do it by the government', her decision to leave teaching was not as a result of wanting to escape from the classroom. Fiona had always thought she would teach for five years and then review her position and, co-incidentally, five years after qualifying she saw an advertisement for and was offered some freelance work at the *TES*. She now works there full time.

At the *TES*, Fiona has moved from sub-editing part of the website to become the editor for new teachers. This encompasses editing the 'First Appointments' supplement for student teachers, commissioning writers, editing articles and putting the supplement together. She also launched the *TES Extra* newsletter for new teachers in September 2003.

How much of Fiona's career progress is owed to her teaching experience?
Fiona's experience as a teacher has proved to be doubly beneficial. As well as developing skills vital for journalism, it has given her an important insight into the *TES*'s audience. 'I'm able to think creatively and on my feet. I can also understand where teachers are coming from – their in-school jokes and what actually matters to them.'

Is the grass greener on the other side?

Fiona has found that working for the *TES* has been more rewarding than teaching in two key ways – pay and flexibility. She currently earns around £40,000 and has also found that there is a greater understanding that 'work can't always come first. One of the great myths about teaching is that it's family friendly, yet in term-time, you are tied to school. Time off for a sick kid, a broken boiler or the school play isn't always possible to negotiate – it depends on your Head.' Nevertheless, she does say, 'I've been lucky. It's easy to get stuck on the same desk but I've had the chance to take on new projects. I'd like to spend more time in schools, though – I miss teaching.'

Fiona's advice

'Explore all your options in and out of the profession. You don't have to remain in the classroom. Maybe you could take a year out and work abroad. I loved supply work and peripatetic teaching – is it possible for you? Whatever you do, don't stay in the same job and whinge until retirement.'

If you are serious about developing yourself as a journalist, she suggests that you start practising while you are teaching and points out the opportunities available to do this at the *TES*. 'I've commissioned a lot of teachers – the *TES* encourages participation from its readership. Send in comment pieces and feature ideas. Read the paper closely and see what you think would be interesting or useful for teachers to read.'

Science and pharmaceutical education management and school liaison 9

Breaking in

A variety of organisations within the science and pharmaceutical sector work with schools to develop and enhance the teaching and learning of science. Larger organisations do have education teams and your experience and knowledge as either a secondary Science teacher or a primary Science co-ordinator (depending on the extent to which science formed part of your undergraduate degree) could be highly regarded.

To enhance your chances of breaking in to this area of work, ensure you follow developments within science education and research. Membership of and activity within science education organisations would also be beneficial, as would secondments or work-shadowing opportunities in the sector. If this is not possible, consider how you might develop educational links within the sector and begin to build up a network of contacts.

Case Study

Siobhan Seymour
Schools Liaison Co-ordinator with a large pharmaceutical organisation

Siobhan qualified as a secondary Science teacher in 1996 and taught in one comprehensive school until 1999.

How did Siobhan get there?
In the first instance, Siobhan was seconded to the post of Schools Liaison Co-ordinator. 'I left teaching initially for one year to be in my current role (on secondment), it was then extended to two years then three, then four! I am now in my fifth year at my current company.'

Siobhan's role entails:

> 'The implementation, co-ordination and evaluation of the schools liaison programme. The programme includes work experience, Nuffield bursaries, primary school workshops, secondary school events, staff training and events and presentations on topics such as the use of animals in medical research.'

How much of Siobhan's career progress is owed to her teaching experience?

Siobhan feels her experience as a teacher has been instrumental in both gaining her current post and carrying out the role.

> 'The company decided to employ a former teacher to co-ordinate the schools programme as the skills, knowledge and experience I brought to the role were unavailable from within the company. Without teaching experience, the programme ran into difficulties, i.e. workshops were above the level of the age of the students and activities were inappropriate.'

Is the grass greener on the other side?

Siobhan is much happier in her current role. 'I am a better schools liaison co-ordinator than I ever was a teacher.'

Siobhan's advice

First and foremost, ask yourself why you want to change career. 'Too often in my field, teachers leave and within a couple of years are teaching again.'

Siobhan's key tips are:

★ 'Make sure your CV is up to date, particularly with regard to IT training, and that it relates to what the employer is looking for. Emphasise project management skills, negotiation skills, time management, team playing and communications experience. Covering letters should also emphasise these details.'

★ 'Interviews are different from those for teaching posts. Psychometric tests are common. Presentations are also included: make sure PowerPoint is used effectively –

employers do not like to see how flashy a presentation can be, i.e. sounds and animation!'

★ 'Choose a career that will enable progression through management levels.'

Case Study

Jane Jones
Head of Education, Association of the British Pharmaceutical Industry (ABPI)

While teaching Science in a grammar school from 1992 to 2000, Jane also held various positions of responsibility, including Head of Year and Key Stage 3 Science Co-ordinator. Her first post on leaving teaching was Education Executive, ABPI

How did Jane get there?

Jane had worked in pharmaceutical research before taking a break to have a family. She trained as a teacher because, she felt, 'teaching would allow me to pass on my enthusiasm for science and also allow me to spend school holidays at home with my children.'

Jane found many aspects of teaching fulfilling: 'enthusiastic pupils, wonderful colleagues and an innovative A-level course in particular.' Although she disliked some elements of teaching, particularly the amount of preparation and marking, she did not seek alternative employment. Her decision to leave was only really in response to seeing a post advertised in the *TES*, which was 'exactly right for me'.

Jane's first post at the ABPI saw her pay increase by around £4,000, followed by further significant rises in her first two years. She reported to the Director of Science and her responsibilities included:

> 'Developing resources to support teaching, providing information on careers in the industry to young people, supporting, encouraging education outreach from our member companies and providing secretarial support for the Education Committee.'

What can I do with... a teaching qualification?

Since becoming Head of Education, her hours and pay have both increased slightly. In addition to the roles described above, she provides support to another committee and has responsibility for higher education liaison. 'A large part of my work in this area has been to develop responses to government consultations on HE.'

How much of Jane's career progress is owed to her teaching experience?

The person specification for Jane's first job with the ABPI said the post was for someone who had both been a teacher and had also worked in the pharmaceutical industry. She regards her teaching experience as being very important:

'I meet teachers, advisers and teacher trainers in the course of my work and would have no credibility with them if I had not taught. I need to fully understand the school system and exam specifications in order to provide and sponsor appropriate teaching materials.'

Is the grass greener on the other side?

In material terms, Jane enjoys better pay, greater flexibility and shorter working hours at the ABPI. However, the enjoyment of her role stems more from the intrinsic satisfaction her work brings.

'I can make more of a difference, e.g. through working on steering groups to develop new qualifications (Science for the 21st Century GCSE, Applied Science GCSE and A-level).

'I enjoy excellent relationships with professional bodies, science organisations, education officers in member companies – interesting people within the network of supporting science education.'

Jane's advice

Jane highlights the importance of actively networking within science organisations.

'Join science organisations (Association of Science Education, Royal Society of Chemistry, etc.) and take an active part, e.g. go to the ASE conference to meet and talk to those working in science-related organisations.

'Read the *TES* and possibly get involved in writing for new courses. Again, you will make contacts and know what's going on.'

'Take on responsibilities at school that will be relevant to what you want to do. Get involved in Education Business Partnership activities and try to develop links with local companies. Develop excellent IT skills, e.g. advanced PowerPoint, Access and Excel and gain experience of managing a budget, possibly outside school.'

Case Study

Dr Colin Osborne
Education Manager, Schools and Colleges, Royal Society of Chemistry (RSC)

Colin taught secondary Science for 24 years in two comprehensive schools. He held the post of Head of Department before moving to the RSC in 1996.

How did Colin get there?
Like Jane, Colin moved into teaching from another career, but in his case this was in industrial property rights. He enjoyed the chance teaching gave him to have daily involvement with science as well as working with pleasant students. In contrast, he disliked 'long hours, stress, too much paperwork, not enough concentration on teaching, lack of support from parents and unpleasant students.'

Colin's and Jane's experience demonstrate how useful it is to keep an eye on non-teaching appointments in education publications. He was not actively seeking a career change but took the opportunity for an 'even better career in an education-related field at a higher salary' after seeing his current post advertised. While the process may seem straightforward, Colin admits that he did face the challenge of 'realising I had the capability to do it since it required skills and knowledge I didn't have, like managing the production of books.'

As Education Manager, in theory Colin works a 37-hour week and earns a salary equivalent to an Advanced Skills teacher. He

What can I do with... a teaching qualification?

supervises eight staff and is responsible for the RSC's programme for schools with a budget of £1 million. Colin says, 'My work involves curriculum materials, courses for teachers, careers material, advice to government and liaison with members.'

How much of Colin's career progress is owed to his teaching experience?

Colin feels that his teaching experience was extremely relevant in gaining his post at the RSC.

> 'An important part of the job is the establishing of credibility with teachers so they believe the organisation is doing the right thing for them. My teaching experience has allowed me to develop the role and become a driver for change.'

In terms of the skills gained from teaching that are relevant to his role, Colin has the following comments.

> 'Almost all of them have been useful, especially presenting to people. Managers have reported that presentations to "the great and the good" have been authoritative and confident and feedback from training of teachers and colleagues within the organisation has been positive.'

Is the grass greener on the other side?

Colin appreciates the increase in salary and reduction in stress in his work at the RSC, as well as the varied work, which has afforded him the opportunity for foreign travel. He does, however, point out that he needs to 'juggle the demands of many projects, meetings and electronic communication in the short-term as well as ensuring long term deliverables are met'.

Colin's advice

Colin advises you to ensure you do really want to leave teaching and that you won't miss the contact with young people. He also emphasises the importance of involvement with subject associations and learned societies and 'working informally with the organisation first, if possible'.

82

Information technology 10

IT Trainer

Breaking in

Information and Communication Technology (ICT) has become a central part of teaching and learning and there are a number of organisations that provide ICT support and expertise to schools.

Qualifications, Experience and Skills

IT trainers may offer support with desktop applications or technical systems. Unless you have had direct experience of working with the technical aspects of IT, the easiest route into IT training is likely to be through training and supporting off-the-shelf packages or tailor-made applications for particular teaching and learning and school management strategies. If you have had *considerable* experience of using, maintaining and supporting IT (perhaps through managing your school's computer network), it may also be worth investigating the possibility of IT training outside the education sector.

A teaching qualification will certainly help you get into IT training in educational settings, but you also need to demonstrate that you have relevant experience and skills. These might be:

★ experience of software packages (and their use within schools)
★ training and support of colleagues
★ ability to analyse training needs
★ patience and the ability to motivate others to learn.

Onwards and Upwards

IT is still a growth area within education, even if the IT sector itself seems to be struggling at the moment. Your career may progress upwards through the management hierarchy of an organisation (although many organisations are relatively small) or onwards through developing greater technical expertise.

Case Study

Nathan Butler-Broad
IT Trainer, CfBT (Centre for British Teachers)

Nathan taught in two primary schools over three years before leaving the profession in 2002. He was also IT, PE and Art Co-ordinator.

How did Nathan get there?
While he enjoyed a great deal of his role, and still finds himself 'pining' to be back in the classroom from time to time, Nathan felt frustrated at the pressure of having limited time to complete many different tasks and activities outside the classroom. He also felt it was important 'to try something new before it was too late'.

He did have some concerns when he first considered moving out of teaching:

> 'The uncertainty of what I was doing and where my career was leading. One thing about teaching is that there is a well-ordered career progression. Life in the outside world seemed a little more open. I also questioned my options – what else could I realistically do with the skills I had. Although highly trained, I had no specific business skills.'

Fortunately, a friend mentioned to Nathan that he had seen the perfect job for him at CfBT. CfBT is an educational management company whose main projects include primary and secondary strategy training, Connexions and work with two LEAs. Nathan's role involves providing training to members of CfBT staff and teachers on all Microsoft Office packages as well as customised databases, designed in-house by CfBT to aid school management.

'I work closely with Regional Directors of the national strategies [literacy, numeracy, Key Stage 3]. A recent development has been to work alongside the new Interactive Whiteboard and Computers and Laptops projects, helping to deliver consultant training in an IT support/advisory role. This is certainly an aspect of my work that I enjoy as it utilises my educational experience and training.'

How much of Nathan's career progress is owed to his teaching experience?

Nathan believes that his teaching experience was fundamental in gaining his job as an IT trainer. 'It proved that I could deliver knowledge to others and that I was hardworking. I work for an educational management company and this experience of school was something they valued.'

Is the grass greener on the other side?

Nathan misses the variety of work in primary school teaching. However, despite fewer holidays, as someone with a young family he has found his new job gives him a better work–life balance.

After just over a year out of teaching, Nathan has decided to return to the classroom:

'I've decided teaching is what I do best and ultimately what I enjoy. The experience out of teaching has given me this perspective and I would still recommend it to anyone looking to develop their skills. I've learnt a lot, mostly about myself, and I believe I'm returning with renewed enthusiasm and determination.'

Nathan's advice

Nathan stresses that when changing career, teachers need to keep their options open in order to ensure they don't miss out on any opportunities. He also points out that you should 'be prepared to find the whole experience slightly strange, particularly in the beginning'.

If you are interested in working as an IT trainer, Nathan has the following tips:

- don't be put off – 'the IT skills which I possess are far greater now than before and have been relatively easy to pick up along the way'
- a basic qualification such as the ECDL (European Computer Driving Licence) could be helpful.

New Media Specialists

Breaking in

CD-ROMS, websites and DVDs are becoming increasingly important in providing learning opportunities in both formal and informal education. Most new media agencies are based in London and the South East.

Experience and Skills

It is important that you are able to demonstrate understanding and experience of the role of new media in education. Contributing to on-line services run for teachers by teachers such as teachers-online.co.uk, using and developing digital curriculum resources and designing your school websites are all useful. You will need to show evidence of:

- awareness of how resources and ideas might be transformed into a format that suits different forms of digital media
- familiarity with computer-based design packages
- creative flair in developing learning resources
- the ability to pitch new ideas to senior managers
- the ability to understand the needs of users, from pupils to parents, from job-seekers to LEA directors
- organisation, self-discipline and the ability to work to tight deadlines
- teamwork skills.

Onwards and Upwards

Career development could be through developing your technical or creative expertise, managing projects or setting up your own business. Salaries in new media for someone with relatively little experience are around £15,000 nationally and £17,000 in London. However, you should be able to use your experience as an educational professional to demand a higher salary if your work is to be within e-learning. Non-managerial new media jobs advertised on totaljobs.com in autumn 2003 offered salaries between £14,000 and £35,000.

Case Study

Carolyn Royston
Head of E-learning, Atticmedia

Carolyn taught for three years in one primary school and held an ICT Co-ordinator role. On leaving teaching she became Education Director with an independent new media company in the West Midlands.

How did Carolyn get there?
Carolyn retrained as a teacher after some years working in publishing. 'I always wanted to teach but drifted into other things.' She found working with children fulfilling – 'being involved in children's lives was challenging and interesting', but she also found that the work was 'never-ending – not just in terms of planning but also emotionally.' Entering the profession as a career-changer presented further challenges to Carolyn in terms of the time it seemed it would take to rebuild her income.

The time lapse between deciding to seek alternative employment and gaining a post outside teaching was about half a term. Having already changed career once, Carolyn admits that leaving teaching and moving back to the private sector 'was not a great leap of faith'. She explains:

'I was lucky. A friend who worked for a new media agency on an education project but who knew very little about education asked me for advice. Initially, I offered this for free and then other projects emerged, eventually leading to full-time work. I began by giving educational input into tenders and then became more involved in content. Basically, I was able to develop the role myself.'

As Head of E-learning for AtticLearning, the education arm of Atticmedia, Carolyn's work shares many similarities with her previous role and she has maintained the freedom to develop her role as she sees fit. She is involved in all aspects of project development, from preparing bids for tenders to content design and implementation. With AtticLearning, Carolyn develops e-learning services for both formal and informal education, developing curriculum-based sites to be used by schools and colleges and heritage sites for organisations, such as the Trade Union Congress Library, and other organisations in the public, voluntary and private sectors.

Recent projects have included a website to support CBBC's Tracy Beaker series (www.bbc.co.uk/cbbc/tracybeaker/), nominated for a New Media Effectiveness Award, developing a series of CD-ROMs for the Institute of Physics' Supporting Physics 11-14 project and the Connexions-Direct Jobs4u database (www.connexions-direct.com/jobs4u/).

In heritage work, Carolyn regards her and her team's expertise as vital in helping museums to transfer 'content suitable for written form into content suitable for the Web'.

How much of Carolyn's career progress is owed to her teaching experience?
Carolyn's education expertise has proved to be an effective marketing tool for AtticLearning. Their website refers to her as their 'in-house educational specialist who has extensive experience of working in the heritage sector'. Carolyn herself reflects:

> 'I have no regrets at all about being a teacher. My teaching experience has been critical for my work. There hasn't been a single project where the fact that I have been a primary school teacher hasn't been mentioned in a positive way – it gives people confidence. I am also grateful to teaching for enhancing the skills that I use currently at work – organisation, teambuilding, and dealing with people.'

Is the grass greener on the other side?
There are aspects of teaching that Carolyn misses: 'I miss the human element of teaching. Teaching is very much people-based, whereas my current role is project-based.' Having

benefited from the support of her union as a teacher, she also points out that workers in the new media sector do not tend to be unionised. Like other teachers she also stresses that you don't get the same 'sense of accomplishment and pride'.

Additionally, compared to teaching, Carolyn sometimes feels her work can be repetitive. 'You may have lots of bad days in teaching but a day is never the same as the day before. In new media, although the projects you work on vary, the processes you go through are very similar.'

However, just as Carolyn didn't regret being a teacher, she also explains why she has no regrets about developing her career within new media.

'I am paid more than I was as a teacher. My official work hours are from 10 a.m. to 6 p.m., Mondays to Fridays and, although I will often work later than that, it is very rare that I will have to work weekends. I don't take work home with me, practically or emotionally, and I don't feel burdened in the way I felt as a teacher. As a teacher, I felt responsible for 30 pupils and their parents. It's nice to be responsible for just the projects I am working on.'

Carolyn's advice

Carolyn stresses that there are opportunities for teachers within new media and offers the following advice.

★ Do your research: 'Find a list of companies that produce educational software and/or content. Look at websites or CD-ROMs that you have used and find out who produced them, or use a search engine to find educational publishers.'

★ Send speculative CVs to the companies you find, and offer your services in developing or advising on content (perhaps initially on a voluntary basis). 'Your experience may relate to a project the company is working on. This has happened at Atticmedia – a language teacher sent us their CV at the same time that we were bidding for a Spanish project. They helped us with our pitch and we were able to pay them a small fee.'

★ Market yourself carefully. 'Many new media agencies interested in developing an education portfolio won't have an in-house education specialist, so your experience could be a highly valuable commodity. Be pro-active and research the skills they are seeking.'

Case Study

Jon Cardus
Company Director, Digitalsavvy Limited

After qualifying as a secondary Science teacher in 1993, Jon taught in two comprehensives before leaving the profession in 1998. His first post on leaving teaching was as Online Education Co-ordinator, BBC.

How did Jon get there?
Jon became a teacher because 'I wanted a vocation that set challenges and gave the necessary autonomy to be able to find the solutions.' He particularly enjoyed being part of the school community, but gradually found that teaching was 'becoming more a day-job, not a vocation' which he felt was due to 'the relentless chipping away of the professional status of teachers'.

Jon found it difficult to decide to leave the profession and it took him about a year to find a suitable job.

'I started by making a list of all the roles and traits a teacher has and mapping this to the needs of the corporate world. It became clear that the multiple talents required as a teacher make such an individual an extremely valuable "commodity".

'This process raised my self–confidence to a level where I felt I could compete successfully in the world outside teaching. It was then a case of identifying a role which would best suit my experience and simply begin knocking on doors. You continually have to describe how your skills can support the business; in essence you quickly become a very effective salesperson.

'It was necessary to utilise every bit of spare time available to gain outside experience, in my case writing for magazines and TV and the – then developing – online industry (more often than not only for the experience). This built up a network of contacts, some of whom were willing to pay for my contributions. After a 12-month period I had a CV which showed how a teacher's skills are eminently transferable.'

As BBC online education co-ordinator, Jon was responsible for matching the content of the BBC schools website to national curriculum requirements.

'This entailed designing and writing for websites such as Bitesize to ensure an effective balance between audience focus and department strategy. It was interesting how narrow job specifications were compared to that of a practising teacher – the narrower brief allowed time for career development. This opened up an entirely new world of new technologies (as new to the BBC at that time as they were to me!). It was a very exciting time. When I joined there were 25 people: this grew quickly to 250.

'Within this environment there was plenty of opportunity to expand into other areas of interest and within two years I was managing major innovation projects looking at broadband and other emergent technologies.'

After two years as online education co-ordinator, Jon spent a further two years as a content producer, and then took on the role of strategic adviser across the BBC. Early in 2003, he and a colleague decided to set up their own company, Digitalsavvy Limited. 'We develop resources that utilise digital technologies and apply them directly to the needs of teachers and students in the classroom – minimising workload and maximising classroom outcomes.'

How much of Jon's career progress is owed to his teaching experience?
Jon feels that his teaching experience provided a foundation for the rest of his career, particularly in establishing his own business.

'Experiences as a teacher have proved invaluable. Creative thinking, communication skills, planning, development and execution and teamwork are absolute necessities in driving the business. Running your own business requires the multi-faceted skills of the teacher, but the skills which most help include strategic and analytical thinking, the ability to communicate to multiple audiences, tenacity and persuasion.

'Most important, though, is knowledge of the needs of teachers and learning communities. It is only through this that we are able to produce resources which do not add to workload whilst at the same time supporting teachers who wish to use new technologies in their subject areas.'

Is the grass greener on the other side?
Jon worked hard to ensure the pros outweighed the cons when he changed career – 'any career change has to be carefully thought through to maximise benefits and negate potential pitfalls'. He found his work environment at the BBC very different to the one he was used to as a teacher:

'I clearly remember a feeling of culture shock. Working in a building where everything is on tap, everyone has the tools necessary to do their job (high-quality computers and software, email, video-conferencing, telephone, access to arguably the best resources in the world). To have bars, restaurants, and gyms on site was also a new experience – it made working late a pleasure.'

Jon is still reaping the rewards of his career change. He enjoys: 'the freedom to make all your own decisions, meeting and working with a wide range of people in a variety of different environments. Every day is different – one day I can be filming, another writing, editing or working in the classroom supporting teachers.'

Jon's Advice
Jon says that patience and enthusiasm are vital in a successful career change.

★ 'Knock-backs are good – critical reflection will strengthen resolve.'
★ 'Work to your personal strengths – build on your skills and experiences.'
★ 'Ensure that your skill set accurately complements and supports the objectives of your future employers – research a role, know the history and future objectives of your chosen employer.'

If you're thinking about running your own business:

★ 'The benefits include the freedom to choose your own destiny but this cuts both ways – you are entirely responsible for keeping a roof over your head – this is exciting but needs careful planning.'

★ 'It's a very small world – stick to your guns, be clear in communicating your intentions but be prepared to compromise. Always keep your contacts: exciting projects can develop from the briefest of encounters.'

★ 'The media can be a very competitive arena: strategically building on your strengths will ensure you have a solid track record.'

11   Finance

Tax Inspection – Inland Revenue

Qualifications

A second-class honours degree is required for entry to the
Inland Revenue's Tax Inspector training programme. Training is
now through the Technical and Compliance stream of their
Talent Recruitment Programme. There is no age limit and it
does not matter how long ago you graduated.

Experience and Skills

The selection process focuses on competencies rather than
experience. You need to consider how teaching has enhanced
your ability to:

★ plan and organise
★ lead and manage people
★ communicate effectively
★ work in teams
★ analyse information and solve problems
★ drive and support change
★ focus on the customer
★ achieve results.

Onwards and Upwards

Technical and Compliance training normally lasts for four
years and aims to prepare trainees for senior management
roles. It is a modular programme combining formal training,
self-study and office-based work, which is assessed through
examination and practical assessment. As you progress
through your training you will move from inspecting tax affairs

of self-employed people to small businesses and more complex work such as corporate tax affairs, choosing a specific business stream for the last year or so of the training.

Career progression could be in a number of areas including policy work and training inspectors. There is also a range of project management and operational management opportunities (see Mary Astley's case study in Chapter 12, Management).

The Inland Revenue is not the only organisation to employ tax specialists. In the public sector, there are also opportunities in HM Treasury and HM Customs and Excise. Further openings might also be found within private sector companies such as PricewaterhouseCoopers, KPMG and Ernst and Young.

On entry to the training programme, trainees receive a salary of £17,510–£18,760 (£20,330–£21,580 in London). On successful completion of training, you can expect to move on to a salary scale of £37,630–£47,590 (£42,250–£54,170 in London). A Senior Civil Servant (SCS) may earn between £69,500 and £121,000 if they reach the 'progression target rate' for their pay band. (In April 2002, 3,540 civil servants were defined as Senior Civil Servants. Under one per cent of Inland Revenue members of staff were earning over £70,000.)

Case Study

Nicola Young
Trainer of Tax Inspectors, Inland Revenue

Nicola taught Latin, Ancient History, Greek and Classical Studies for 12 years in two secondary schools. On leaving teaching she became a Trainee Tax Inspector.

How did Nicola get there?
Nicola says she became a teacher because, 'I loved my subject and wanted to share my enthusiasm. I always enjoyed explaining things and I've always been a bit of a "performer".'

She does have happy memories of teaching: 'I liked the children – we had fun in the lessons. It was good to continue studying my subject.'

Despite the elements of teaching she enjoyed, Nicola began to experience an increasing burden of work and 'an increasing lack of respect and courtesy from staff and children.' The advent of the National Curriculum made it difficult to teach her specialism in a state school.

'It was time for a change. It took me three to four months to obtain a job outside teaching. I had a careers interview at my former university, applied to an advert and got the job. Ironically, this was much easier than finding my first teaching job!'

Nicola was offered a place on the Inland Revenue's Inspector Graduate Training Programme, which lasted for four years and took her to civil service Grade 7, which is senior management level. She is now a Trainer of Inspectors.

'As a fully fledged inspector, I initially worked in a small South London office where I gained a broad experience, including management. I was then based in central London in a similar but more challenging role working with larger businesses before becoming a trainer in 1998. I am known as a 'learning specialist', delivering training to inspectors, mostly on examination courses but also on week-long courses. I have just moved into a new role, maintaining and updating Capital Gains Tax training resources which requires me to keep up to date with legislation and develop materials and case studies.'

How much of Nicola's career progress is owed to her teaching experience?
Although she doesn't regard her teaching experience as being fundamental in her selection as a Trainee Tax Inspector, Nicola points out, 'many teachers got through the selection process. The ability to think on one's feet and the life experience gained from teaching were instrumental in our success.' Nicola feels that her experience has been of real value in her current role:

'I am very interested in testing and exams and would regard my training style to be akin to that of a sixth form teacher. I use many teaching techniques and I'm very syllabus focused, organised and disciplined. I've received positive feedback from trainees about my style as they feel they "know where they are".'

Nicola feels that the skills she developed as a teacher that have been particularly useful are:

★ timing and planning training sessions
★ explaining concepts and processes to groups
★ marking and giving feedback.

Is the grass greener on the other side?
Nicola does not regard her current role as having any disadvantages when compared to teaching. 'Remaining in the public sector can be a good move for teachers as you are able to maintain a public service ethic. The job is generally less stressful and you have a lot more autonomy in the training as long as you get through the syllabus before the exam.'

She also points out:

★ the salary at Grade 7 and above in the civil service compares favourably with teaching
★ it is rare to have to work at home
★ 'you receive much more respect from colleagues.'

Nicola's advice
Nicola has the following reflections on her career change.

'My success was due to a combination of luck and organisation. I felt I had nothing to lose, which gave me greater confidence in front of the interview panel and I was very conscious of the advantages of my life experience compared to new graduates going through the selection process with me.'

Nicola stresses the importance of thinking carefully about what you have to offer a potential employer. She says:

★ 'don't underestimate yourself and your personal attributes'
★ 'analyse your skills and qualities before you start'

★ consult a careers professional – 'I visited a careers adviser at the university where I did my second degree, which was very helpful. It helped me to focus on which areas to aim for.'

National Audit Office Auditor

Breaking in

The National Audit Office (NAO) is responsible for the financial and 'value for money' audit of central government departments, agencies and other bodies. It audits over 600 government accounts every year. Its role is to assess whether these accounts are free from material misstatements and to decide whether their transactions have parliamentary authority.

Qualifications

Recruits to the NAO must have at least a 2:1 in any degree discipline and GCSEs or O levels in English and Maths. At least 24 UCAS points are required, but this may be waived for applicants over 25.

Experience and Skills

The transferable skills you will need to demonstrate include:

★ high level of numeracy – this will be assessed through a Test of Mathematical Competence (TMC)
★ organisation and time management skills
★ the ability to absorb, analyse and present information to other people
★ an eye for detail
★ communication with a range of people at different levels and with different abilities.

Onwards and Upwards

Through the NAO's graduate training programme, trainees study towards the Associate Chartered Accountant (ACA)

exams necessary to become a member of the Institute of
Chartered Accountants in England and Wales (ICAEW) and
to assume the title of Chartered Accountant.

Starting salaries in London are £21,912, rising throughout
training to reflect exam success. Completion of the training
normally leads to promotion to Senior Auditor, placing staff on
a salary of more than £37,000. As with the civil service, staff
also benefit from a non-contributory pension.

On completion of the training and having gained entry to the
ICAEW, NAO staff are able to develop their careers in a
variety of ways, whether within financial auditing or in 'value
for money' work. There are also opportunities for secondment
elsewhere in the public sector or in the private sector. Career
development may also involve taking on more managerial roles
or planning and delivering training.

As the ACA is a portable qualification, it is also possible to
develop an accountancy career in the private sector. Value for
money work shares a lot in common with management
accountancy and such specialists may find further
opportunities in the public and private sector as well as
through offering freelance services.

Case Study

Martine James
Principal Auditor, National Audit Office

Martine taught PE and Maths in two middle schools between
1989 and 1998 and held the positions of PE Co-ordinator (one
term) and Head of Maths. Her first post on leaving teaching
was Assistant Auditor, National Audit Office.

How did Martine get there?
Martine got great job satisfaction from teaching but towards the
end of her time as a teacher she became increasingly frustrated
with 'the level of testing and emphasis on league tables for

English, Mathematics and Science. The formalisation of lesson structures was also removing the opportunity to be creative.'

Martine started her search for a new career by 'looking in the broadsheet national newspapers for adverts, talking to people about their careers to find out what was of interest to me and visiting careers services to do research.'

Once she made the decision to leave the profession it took Martine about a year to find a job. She says her biggest challenge was 'convincing an employer that someone approaching 30 years of age was capable of being retrained and that it was a worthwhile investment.'

Martine joined the National Audit Office in 1998, one of a cohort of over 30 trainees, including a number of other mature entrants embarking on a new career.

'I joined on a three-year training contract as an Assistant Auditor, studying for a Chartered Accountancy qualification on block release.

'When not at training college, my job was to work in a team of around 15 people, including another recruit, conducting the financial audit of the Department for Education and Employment and its related bodies. This involved visiting regional offices, checking transactions and assets and interviewing staff, with the aim of ascertaining whether systems were robust and financial transactions were recorded correctly.

'Although my salary level was initially considerably lower than that as a teacher, the arrangements for my pension contributions meant that my monthly net income was not drastically reduced. I also had the prospect of significant salary rises as I successfully completed elements of my training.'

During the latter part of Martine's training, she was involved in more complex audits. 'Before the end of my training contract I was planning and running audits of organisations with annual expenditure of five billion pounds.' In the two years since completing training she has been promoted twice. She is now a

Principal Auditor and is responsible for managing staff, particularly trainee auditors. She estimates that her salary is 50 per cent higher than it would have been had she remained a teacher.

Martine now specialises in value for money audit:

'This is more akin to management consultancy work, where we conduct one-off examinations of certain aspects of government activity, and recommend ways that it might be done more economically, efficiently and effectively. I work on the health area, examining such topics as health and safety in NHS trusts and accident and emergency services.'

Some of Martine's key responsibilities include:

★ 'Leading the fieldwork tasks and documenting and submitting results of investigations.'
★ 'Allocating audit tasks to team members and reviewing their outputs.'
★ 'Contributing to briefings and reports of the Committee of Public Accounts.'
★ 'Representing the NAO with clients at all levels.'
★ 'Supervising trainees and assessing their performance, including planning for the development of their potential.'
★ 'Over the last 18 months, I have also become increasingly involved in office-wide training activities. I conduct training courses (or individual sessions) for new recruits and staff from overseas audit offices.'

How much of Martine's career progress is owed to her teaching experience?

Martine feels being a teacher prepared her for her work at the NAO in the following ways.

★ 'I am drawing heavily on my teaching experience. I often conduct training alongside colleagues who have a great deal of audit knowledge and experience, but whose training skills have been self-learnt. By applying my knowledge of teaching theory and practice, I have been able to design and deliver better training courses.'
★ 'Having been a teacher I am used to absorbing, analysing and presenting information to other people and this has

helped me through my examinations and with my role in liaising with clients.'

- 'My experience of working with pupils has been useful when looking for inconsistencies in paperwork and interpreting body language in interviews. Developing strategies for dealing with difficult pupils has equipped me to handle defensive or awkward clients.'
- 'Management responsibilities are an integral part of teaching from day one. This prepared me extremely well for my current job and I have the reputation for being organised and capable of managing my time and that of others effectively.'

Is the grass greener on the other side?

Although Martine misses some of the autonomy she had as a teacher, she regards her current job as having the following advantages over teaching:

- 'Governmental interference is not a factor and the goalposts are not constantly being moved.'
- 'I can leave my work at my desk to a greater extent – I can still wake up at night with issues that are dominating my thoughts but I'm not always thinking how I could incorporate a new experience I've had into my lesson plans.'
- 'If I'm really unwell I don't need to feel guilty about someone else having to pick up my work – it'll still be there for me when I return and people don't have to use their time to cover my absence.'

Martine's advice

- 'Be prepared that retraining might involve long hours and a lot of effort. You'll probably need to start in quite a junior role and work your way up, so look for a nationally recognised qualification to maximise the benefits and opportunities of the retraining.'
- 'Look for organisations that have a track record in employing graduates other than those who have just left university.'
- 'Aim to complete your Chartered qualification before you are 35 years old. Try to get a contract that entitles you to study leave and blocks of college tuition. Studying as well as holding down a full-time job is exceptionally demanding.'
- 'Think carefully about whether relocation is a possibility and whether travel away from home is an acceptable part of your

working life. Audits around the country are usual and commuting daily isn't always an option.'

Case Study

Susannah Drazin
Assistant Auditor, National Audit Office

Susannah taught Maths in two secondary schools between 1992 and 2000, and held a number of positions of responsibility.

How did Susannah get there?
Susannah loved teaching Maths but a variety of reasons, including workload and a lack of resources, as well as ill-health, led her to leave the profession.

Susannah describes her biggest challenge in finding work as, 'I just didn't know what my options were or what I wanted to do.' After taking some time out, she started to consider her career options. 'I went to a job fair at Olympia and picked up leaflets and talked to people. This was more helpful in ruling stuff out than actually giving me ideas (although I did find out about my current place of work there).'

Susannah also visited a local authority careers service where she was recommended to join an EU-funded job-seeking programme. Through this programme she spent three days at a firm of actuaries. Although she ruled out training as an actuary because it would take too long to qualify, Susannah found that this experience 'enabled me to get a proper feel for office life and talk to other people.'

Susannah is now in the middle of her three-year training contract at the NAO, conducting a variety of financial audit work. As well as studying for the ICAEW qualification, she also attends the NAO's internal training programme.

What can I do with... a teaching qualification?

How much of Susannah's success is due to her teaching experience?

Susannah found her teaching experience was useful during her interviews for the NAO training programme: 'teaching has given me presentation skills, which helped at the interview'.

She has also found the following skills useful in her current role:

★ time-keeping
★ talking to people
★ report-writing
★ presentations.

Is the grass greener on the other side?

'I took a considerable drop in salary when I took this job. I was on £32,000 in teaching and I'm now on just over £20,000. However, it took me nine years to get to £32,000 in teaching whereas I should be able to do it in four in this job.'

Although she misses the fun of teaching and doesn't particularly enjoy working away from home and doing exams, Susannah recognises that the culture and environment at the NAO is more conducive to performing well but without the pressure of working long hours.

Susannah's advice

Susannah has these tips for teachers considering a career change:

★ 'Don't procrastinate, make the decision and go.'
★ 'Rewrite your CV so that it emphasises skills rather than experience.'
★ 'Know why you want to leave so that you don't end up in another job with the same problems.'
★ 'Talk to the careers teacher in your school; they'll have books and leaflets and computer programs that can help.'
★ 'Make sure you have a pat answer when people ask why you left – they will ask you continually.'

Susannah also stresses the need to consider the impact of studying for professional qualifications. 'The exams are not like other exams you will have done. They are not that difficult intellectually but they are very intense and time pressured. Make sure that you have the support and understanding of your family to get you through these.'

12 Management – moving up

In this chapter there are just a few examples of how former teachers have progressed upwards within the organisations in which they work. For some of them, success has developed over some years, and for others, advancement has followed relatively quickly after leaving teaching.

Case Study

Anwyn Stephenson
Customer Services Manager, Edexcel

Anwyn qualified as a secondary business studies teacher in Scotland in 1994. She taught in a sixth-form college and comprehensive in England until 2001, where she held various positions of responsibility, from GNVQ Co-ordinator to Head of Business Studies and ICT Faculty. Her first post on leaving teaching was Assessment Leader, Edexcel.

How did Anwyn get there?
Anwyn became a teacher because she enjoyed the subjects she trained to teach and because she wanted a job that was 'worthwhile and helped others to progress'. She found many elements of teaching rewarding, particularly working with post-16 students, and 'being involved in the implementation of vocational qualifications and seeing students who have underachieved in the past do well in these qualifications.'

However, Anwyn began to find aspects of the job frustrating, from students' apathy to lack of support from senior management and the feeling that there was a general lack of respect for education in England. Furthermore, she says:

'I was given lots of promotions while I was still young. As a result there seemed to be nowhere left for me to go. The next step up was senior management, and I did apply for some assistant headship posts, but I felt the fact that I had only a few years of teaching experience seemed to be preventing me from being interviewed.'

While applying for senior management posts, Anwyn also applied for and was offered an Assessment Leader post at Edexcel, which she held for 12 months.

'I was appointed Assessment Leader for A-level Economics and Economics/Business and took over the role of Assessment Leader for GNVQ/VCE Business. I was responsible for question-paper production and administering the marking of examination papers, managing a team of examiners to ensure a consistency of standards. I led INSET with teachers and helped to develop the qualifications I dealt with.'

Anwyn is now Customer Services Manager, reporting to the Head of Customer Services.

'After appointment as Customer Services Manager, I set up a team with four direct reports. I have been instrumental in providing a focal point for written complaints in Edexcel, setting up a structured complaint process, which has helped to portray the company in a far more professional way.

'I am also responsible for raising customer awareness across the company, root-cause analysis, recruitment and training of new staff, staff development, team building and interdepartmental relationship building.

'I also currently manage the relationship between an outsourcer and Edexcel with specific responsibility for the £2million contract.'

As her career has progressed, Anwyn's salary has increased to a level comparable with a senior management post in teaching and she has had responsibility for managing a team of 16 staff.

How much of Anwyn's career progress is owed to her teaching experience?
Although Anwyn does not regard her teaching experience as being particularly relevant to her current post, she certainly

recognises its role in initially getting her into Edexcel: 'Assessment Leader roles tend to be filled by ex-teachers.' She also acknowledges how useful the skills she developed as a teacher have been in her career progression, pinpointing these transferable skills:

★ interpersonal skills – 'communication, coaching, negotiation, a diplomatic attitude and being able to manage difficult situations'
★ IT skills.

Is the grass greener on the other side?
Like many of the former teachers in this book, Anwyn does miss the holidays but, although she is happy to have remained in the education sector, she is very aware of the benefits of her current role, particularly in terms of her own development. 'I feel that more time and money has been invested in my personal and professional development in the last two years than was ever done in my seven years of teaching.'

Anwyn's advice
Anwyn suggests that you should start learning how to sell yourself by discussing your skills with family, friends and colleagues and encourages you to:

'have confidence in the skills you have developed in teaching but be realistic and talk to a careers adviser. Take a risk – you can always return to teaching – but don't assume people will know the skills you have developed. Make sure you match your skills to the job spec.'

Case Study

Mary Astley
Senior Civil Servant
Mary taught secondary Maths for nine years until the late 1980s. During this time she held the post of deputy head of department. Her first post after leaving teaching was Trainee Tax Inspector.

How did Mary get there?
Mary became a teacher partly because of a lack of careers guidance, but she did enjoy many aspects of the role.

'Compared to my other jobs, it has given me the best highs.' On the other hand, it also gave her 'some of the worst lows', and she left because she began to feel de-motivated by the seeming lack of value placed on the profession at the time.

Mary successfully applied for the Inland Revenue's tax inspector graduate training scheme (see Chapter 11, Finance). She progressed through both sideways and upwards movement.

'I applied for internal vacancies – moving up through grades and taking a variety of posts within grades to broaden my experience. I was earmarked as having management potential and so was given a variety of development opportunities to enhance my experience and knowledge of a breadth of IR functions such as policy work.

'I was asked if I would be interested in my current role in operations management. In this role I am in charge of business delivery and development for one of the Inland Revenue's seven operational units and have line management responsibility for 17 people.'

How much of Mary's career progress is owed to her teaching experience?

Mary suspects that her teaching experience may have played a part in her success: 'I was regarded as having management potential – I'm not sure if this was seen as "natural talent" or based on the experience I had gained through teaching.'

Whatever the basis of her potential, Mary does regard some of the skills she developed as a teacher as being useful in her current position:

★ people-handling skills
★ dealing with confrontation (also developed through tax inspection work)
★ time management – the ability to juggle different priorities.

Is the grass greener on the other side?

While Mary earns considerably more than her friends who have remained in teaching – senior civil servants can earn between £69,500 and £121,000 (see Chapter 11, Finance) – she points out that senior positions bring with them long working hours.

Nevertheless, she still believes that the role is not as tiring as teaching and, although she stresses that it is difficult to compare her current role with teaching, she feels her job has the following advantages:

> 'There seems to be more autonomy and the flexibility to manage your time and deliver work due to the alternative working patterns available within the civil service. Although there is a degree of stress in my role, it is very different to the stress of being responsible for a room full of 30 teenagers – the level of stress perhaps isn't as relentless as it is in teaching.'

Mary's advice
Mary stresses the benefits of working for the civil service and the Inland Revenue in particular. 'It is a good employer – there are plenty of development opportunities, a variety of work and it is possible to manage your own career within the Revenue.'

She emphasises that working for the civil service may sit comfortably with teachers who feel it is important that they are able to contribute to society through their work. If you are interested in the civil service, she suggests you should 'find out about the range of jobs. There are lots of different schemes of entry at different levels (you can start at a lower level if your degree result isn't too good and work your way up) and in different departments.'

Case Study

Alice Lowe
Operations Manager in a Multi-National Chemical and Petroleum Corporation

Alice completed a secondary Science PGCE in the mid-1980s but decided not to teach. She took up a post as Project Manager with an international electronics company.

How did Alice get there?
Alice decided not to teach at the end of her PGCE because, she felt, 'I would restrict my own personal growth. I thought I would spend my life handing on my limited experience at 21 without the opportunity to further develop myself.' Alice's first post involved assisting in applications for government grants,

setting up working groups and co-ordinating financial and technical reporting on projects. Over the next few years she studied part time for an MSc in Manufacturing Systems, and moved to a furniture company with an annual turnover of 40 million pounds, where within five years she was promoted from production controller to factory manager and then operations director, managing 250 staff.

Alice moved to her current company, initially as a management consultant, after taking various MBA modules in 1996.

'I have been significantly involved in managing the transition of business from one company to the company with which it has now been merged in the Middle East. I assist the sector and Middle East-based management in operational aspects of the business. This can cover anything from strategy and planning to performance measurement, organisational design, human resources training and development, financial and management reporting and the mentoring of key staff. My salary is £100,000 plus £15,000 in benefits.'

How much of Alice's career progress is owed to her teaching experience?
Although her career path has taken Alice a long way from teaching, she can still see its relevance in some aspects of her work. 'It has been helpful for the roles that I have had in developing training materials, delivering training and facilitating workshops and working parties.'

Is the grass greener on the other side?
Having been out of teaching for some time, Alice finds it difficult to compare her current role with teaching. She does note, however, that she seems to experience less stress and a higher salary than her peers who are teachers. She also says she appreciates 'the opportunity to take on different types of responsibility through being part of a large firm, working with a wide range of different people and disciplines.'

Alice's advice
As a former teacher and an employer, Alice has the following tip: 'when writing CVs and going to interviews, make sure you understand the *management* skills you have developed as a teacher as these are very valuable to employers.'

References

DfES (2003), *School Workforce in England*

Johnson, M and Hallgartern, J (eds) (2002), *From Victims of Change to Agents of Change: The Future of the Teaching Profession*, IPPR

Penna, Sanders and Sidney (2001), *Taking the Plunge*

Smithers, A and Robinson, P (2001), *Teachers Leaving*, Centre for Education and Employment Research

Useful sources of information

General

TTA – Returning to Teach Information

TTA Returning to Teach, PO Box 3049, Chelmsford CM1 3YT.

Returners' information line: 0845 6000 993; email: returners@teach-tta.gov.uk; website: www.useyourheadteach.gov.uk/returning_to_teach/

Booklets

AGCAS, *Teaching Beyond the Classroom*

Websites

Association of Graduate Recruiters: www.agr.org.uk

Council for Industry and Higher Education: www.cihe-uk.com

Guardian Work Unlimited: www.money.guardian.co.uk/work

Prospects Web: www.prospects.ac.uk

Total Jobs: www.totaljobs.com

Trotman Publishing: www.trotmanpublishing.co.uk

Education and Support Outside the Classroom

Newspapers

Guardian – Tuesday (Education), Wednesday (Society)

The Times Educational Supplement

Websites

Association of Educational Psychologists: www.aep.org.uk

British Psychological Society: www.bps.org.uk

Campaign for Learning: www.campaign-for-learning.org.uk

Charity People: www.charitypeople.co.uk

Connexions Practitioners: www.connexions.gov.uk/
    partnerships/

Local Government Careers: www.lgcareers.com

SENCO Forum: http://search.ngfl,gov.uk/senco-forum

TES: www.tes.co.uk

Young People Now: www.ypnmagazine.com

Educational Research

Websites – Research Organisations and Policy Think Tanks

British Educational Research Association: www.bera.ac.uk

European Educational Research Association: www.eera.ac.uk

Institute of Public Policy Research: www.ippr.org.uk

National Foundation for Educational Research:
    www.nfer.ac.uk

Scottish Centre for Research in Education: www.scre.ac.uk

Websites – Teacher Associations

Association for Language Learning: www.languagelearn.co.uk

Association for Science Education: www.ase.org.uk

Association for the Teaching of the Social Sciences:
    www.atss.org.uk

British Association for Early Childhood Education: www.early-education.org.uk

European Association of Teachers: www.aede.org

National Association for Primary Education: www.nape.org.uk

National Association for Special Educational Needs: www.nasen.org.uk

National Literacy Association: www.nla.org.uk

Higher Education Advice, Guidance and Support

Websites

Association of Graduate Careers Advisory Services: www.agcas.org.uk

Learning and Skills Council: www.lsc.gov.uk

Lifelong Learning: www.lifelonglearning.co.uk

National Association for Student Money Advisers: www.nasma.org.uk

UKCOSA – Council for International Education: www.ukcosa.org.uk

Museums

Journals

Museum Practice and *Museums Journal* (Museums Association)

Websites

Museums Association: www.museumsassociation.org

Group for Education in Museums: www.gem.org.uk

Council of Museums in Wales: www.cmw.org.uk

Scottish Museums Council: www.scottishmuseums.org.uk

Northern Ireland Museums Council: www.nimc.org.uk

Information Services, Publishing and Journalism

Websites

Book Careers: www.bookcareers.com

Chartered Institute of Library and Information Professionals: www.cilip.org.uk

Hansard: www.hansard-westminster.co.uk

Institute of Linguists: www.iol.org.uk

Institute of Sales Promotion: www.isp.org.uk

Institute of Translation and Interpreting: www.iti.org.uk

National Council for the Training of Journalists: www.nctj.com

Publishing News: www.publishingnews.co.uk

Science and Pharmaceutical Education Management and School Liaison

Websites

Association of Science Education: www.ase.org.uk

Association of the British Pharmaceutical Industry: www.abpi.org.uk

Royal Society of Chemistry: www.rsc.org.uk

Information Technology

Websites

AtticLearning: www.atticlearning.com

BBC Learning: www.bbc.co.uk/learning

British Educational Communications and Technology Agency: www.becta.org.uk

British Interactive Multimedia Association: www.bima.co.uk

Centre for British Teachers: www.cfbt.com

Digitalsavvy: www.digitalsavvy.co.uk

eLearning Alliance: www.elearningalliance.org.uk

National Grid for Learning: www.ngfl.gov.uk

Teachers Online: www.teachers-online.co.uk

Finance

Websites

Civil Service Recruitment Gateway: www.careers.civil-service.gov.uk

Inland Revenue Talent Recruitment Programme: www.inlandrevenue.gov.uk/talent/

Institute of Chartered Accountants in England and Wales: www.icaew.co.uk

Institute of Chartered Accountants in Ireland: www.icai.ie

Institute of Chartered Accountants of Scotland: www.icas.org.uk

National Audit Office Graduate Recruitment: www.nao.gov.uk/graduates/